2,50

D1225204

THE SONG OF SONGS

TEXTS and STUDIES

of

THE JEWISH THEOLOGICAL SEMINARY OF AMERICA

VOL. XX

THE SONG OF SONGS

A Study, Modern Translation and Commentary

THE SONG OF SONGS
A Study, Modern Translation and Commentary

by

ROBERT GORDIS

NEW YORK

THE JEWISH THEOLOGICAL SEMINARY OF AMERICA

5714 - 1954

Copyright, 1954, by

ROBERT GORDIS

TABLE OF CONTENTS

FOREWORD

Books have their own peculiar destinies, a Latin proverb informs us. Every student of human nature knows how wide are the fluctuations in fashion and interest affecting men's attitudes toward works of literature, art and music.

In this regard, the *Song of Songs* is a shining exception. For over twenty centuries it has retained its appeal to men's hearts. To be sure, the book has been variously interpreted during its long career. Earlier ages, perhaps more devout than our own, read the *Song of Songs* as an allegory and saw in it an expression of the ideal relationship of love subsisting between God and man. However, as the full scope and character of Biblical literature became evident, this traditional view, in spite of its inherent charm and religious significance, became less and less popular and is today virtually abandoned. Within the last few decades, the allegorical theory has been revived in a very special form. Some scholars have sought to interpret the *Song* as the ritual of a pagan fertility-cult, but this effort cannot be pronounced a success, as this study seeks to demonstrate.

Today it is generally recognized that the book is to be understood literally, its theme being human love, a view which was, indeed, adumbrated in ancient times. Yet even now there is no unanimity with regard to the meaning and character of the book. Some scholars have maintained the position that the book is a drama, with either two or three characters. This theory is still frequently encountered in popular treatments of the *Song*, but it, too, I believe, cannot sustain critical examination.

As the results of archaeological and literary research continue to mount, it becomes increasingly clear that the *Song* cannot be understood in isolation, however splendid and exalted. The life and faith of ancient Israel is, on the one hand, part of the culture-pattern of the ancient Near East and, on the other, markedly distinct from it. Unless both elements of this ambivalent yet perfectly natural relationship are fully taken into account, we obtain a distorted picture of reality.

ix

Only when the Bible is set within the larger framework of the Fertile Crescent, can we gain an adequate appreciation both of its place in the world from which it emerged and of its unique character. For it is both the record of God's revelation to man and of man's aspiration toward the Divine.

When the *Song of Songs* is studied without preconceived notions, it emerges as a superb lyrical anthology, containing songs of love and nature, of courtship and marriage, emanating from at least five centuries of Hebrew history, from the days of Solomon to the Persian period. The *Song* thus constitutes a parallel, though of considerably smaller compass, to the *Book of Psalms,* which is a florilegium of man's yearning and love for God. If the two basic imperatives of religion are the love of God and the love of man, the *Song of Songs,* no less than the *Book of Psalms,* deserves its place in Scripture.

Nor is this all. John MacMurray has written that "the Hebrew form of thought rebels against the very idea of a distinction between the secular and the religious aspects of life." This acute observation does not go far enough. Authentic Hebrew thought did not rebel against the dichotomy; it never recognized its existence. The inclusion of the *Song of Songs* in the Biblical canon is evidence of the persistence in Judaism of the basic conception that the natural is holy, being the manifestation of the Divine. On this score, too, the *Song of Songs,* to borrow Akiba's phrase, is the Holy of Holies.

A word on the scope of the present work is perhaps in order. The Introduction traces the history of the interpretation of the *Song* and presents the conclusions as to the nature and content of the book, which have commended themselves to me on the basis of long study. The technical question of date is difficult to establish in a lyrical work, but fortunately is not basic to its appreciation. On the other hand, it is essential to determine the extent and meaning of each component song in the collection, besides indicating the significance of the work as a whole. For the *Song* is an integral element in the world-view of ancient Israel, to which modern men are justly turning in increasing measure. All these aspects are treated briefly in the Introduction. A fresh Translation of the Hebrew text with a prefatory comment on each song then follows, which, it is hoped, will make the book both intelligible and attractive to the general, non-technical reader. This version is followed by the philological and textual Commentary, which sets forth the grounds for the various positions adopted in the Translation.

From this summary, the reader may recognize that the present study follows the general pattern of the author's previous work, *Koheleth—The Man and His World* (New York, 1951). That it is considerably briefer is due to several reasons. In the first instance, the interpretation of the *Song of Songs*, both as a whole and in detail, offers much less difficulty than that of *Ecclesiastes*. In the second, my approach to the style, structure and content of *Koheleth* was largely unique, though I am happy to note that it has won considerable support since the publication of the book. Because of its originality, my standpoint in *Koheleth* had to be validated at every point against views hitherto prevalent. No such iconoclastic duty faced me in the *Song of Songs*. The basic conception of the book as a collection of lyrics is widely, though not universally, maintained. The task of the interpreter was thus considerably simplified.

While not attempting to exhaust the exegetical literature, I have tried to set forth alternative views which possess merit or interest, particularly on difficult passages. For each student can scarcely hope to do more than make a slight advance in the interpretation of a Biblical book—but this is reward enough. The disregard of the work of others is not only morally indefensible; it is a grave disservice to the cause of truth.

My sincere thanks are extended to President Louis Finkelstein, for including the book in the series of *Texts and Studies of the Jewish Theological Seminary*. Virtually the entire work originally appeared in the *Mordecai M. Kaplan Jubilee Volumes*. I am grateful to my dear colleague, Dr. Moshe Davis, editor of the *Jubilee Volumes*, for including the present study, in spite of its relative length, in the *Festschrift*. It was a privilege to join in a heartfelt tribute to Professor Kaplan, an honored teacher and beloved colleague, whom we admire as a creative thinker of the first magnitude and whom we love for his moral and intellectual integrity.

It is the pleasantest of duties to express heartfelt thanks for the unfailing courtesy and helpfulness of the staffs of three superb libraries in New York City. I am deeply grateful to Columbia University, the Jewish Theological Seminary and the Union Theological Seminary, all of which have not only granted me access to their matchless collections in the fields of Biblical, Judaic and Oriental literature, but have afforded me the stimulus and inspiration of teaching on their distinguished Faculties.

The manifold concerns of an active public career would have ruled out scholarly work completely for me, were I not singularly blessed. The men and women of Temple Beth-El of Rockaway Park, to whom I have ministered, have through the years manifested a genuine understanding and appreciation of scholarship in general and of my own interests in particular, and have thus made it possible for me to engage in teaching and research. My devoted friend, Rabbi Abraham I. Shinedling, has, out of his love of learning and his boundless friendship for the author, proof-read the manuscript and the page-proofs. By his extraordinary knowledge and vigilance, he has contributed greatly to the value and accuracy of the book. My loyal secretary, Mrs. Murray B. Cohen, has done far more than type and retype the manuscript. Her insight, patience and encouragement have long been a tower of strength to me.

Above all, my deepest gratitude is expressed to my dear friend, David Teitelbaum, who has made countless contributions to the welfare of his people and of his fellow-men. His generous gift has made possible the publication of this work as a memorial to his late brother, Sam Teitelbaum. May this book prove a worthy tribute!

The debt I owe my dear wife is not to be put into words. Our twenty-five years of married life have brought us the conviction that the *Song of Songs* is a testament of truth as well as a hymn to joy. This Foreword is being written on the occasion of our Silver Anniversary. As we look toward our golden jubilee, the verse in the *Song of Songs* becomes a prayer in our hearts. "Golden beads shall we make thee, with studs of silver." But our lives are in His hands, and we are content.

ROBERT GORDIS

Belle Harbor, Long Island
February 5, 1953.

THE SONG OF SONGS

I. A Unique Book

"The entire universe is not as worthy as the day on which the Song of Songs was given to Israel, for all the Writings are holy, but the Song of Songs are the Holy of Holies."[1] In these passionate words, Rabbi Akiba was upholding the right of the Song of Songs to a place in the Scriptures. The warmth of his defense testifies to the vigor of the challenge to which it was subjected, probably stronger than in the case of Esther, Koheleth and Job.[2]

The Song of Songs is unique among the books of the Bible in spirit, content and form. It is the only book in the canon lacking a religious or national theme, the Divine name occurring only once and then only as an epithet (8:6). To be sure, Esther also makes no direct mention of God, but its national emphasis is unmistakable. Even that is lacking in the Song of Songs. The reason for the doubts as to its canonicity is not hard to discover. Fragments of secular poetry are imbedded in the Bible,[3] but this is the only complete work which is entirely secular, indeed, sensuous, in character.

As in the case of Koheleth,[4] more than one factor helped to win admission for this little book into the canon of Scripture. While the charm and beauty of its contents played their part, if only on the subconscious level, there were two basic factors operating consciously. First was the occurrence of Solomon's name in the text,[5] which led to the attribution of the whole book to him, as witness the title: "The Song of Songs, which is Solomon's" (1:1). The several references to "the king"[6] were, naturally enough, identified with Solomon as well. Second was the allegorical interpretation of the book, according to which the love of God and Israel is described under the guise of

---

[1] For the entire passage in M. Yad. 3:5, see note 38 below.

[2] On the canonicity of these contested Biblical books, see F. Buhl, *Canon and Text of the O. T.* (Edinburgh, 1892), pp. 3–32; H. E. Ryle, *Canon of the O. T.* (2nd ed., London, 1909); as well as the suggestive treatments of Max L. Margolis, *The Hebrew Scriptures in the Making* (Philadelphia, 1922), pp. 83–96, and S. Zeitlin, "An Historical Study of the Canonization of Hebrew Scriptures," in *Proceedings of the American Academy for Jewish Research*, vol. III (1932), pp. 121–58. See also R. H. Pfeiffer, *Introduction to the O. T.* (New York, 1941), pp. 50–70.

[3] See below, sec. VI.

[4] See R. Gordis, *Koheleth — The Man And His World* (New York, 1951), chap. IV (later referred to as *KMW*).

[5] In 1:1, 5; 3:7, 9, 11; 8:11–12.

[6] In 1:4, 12; 7:6.

a lover and his beloved.[7] This seemed reasonable since wise King Solomon would surely occupy himself only with recondite, spiritual concerns. Hence the Solomonic authorship of the book undoubtedly strengthened, if it did not create, the allegorical interpretation of the Song. This interpretation found Biblical warrant in the frequent use by the Prophets of the metaphor of marital love to describe the proper relationship of Israel to its God.[8] This combination of factors overcame all doubts about the sacred character of the Song of Songs, and its canonicity was reaffirmed at the Council of Jamnia in 90 C. E., never to be seriously challenged again.[9]

II. THE ALLEGORICAL INTERPRETATION

The allegorical view of the Song of Songs to which we owe its inclusion in the canon and therefore its preservation was already well established in the first century C. E. The Apocryphal book *IV Esdras* uses the figures of "lily," "dove," and "bride" to refer to Israel (5:24, 26; 7:26). While the comparison to a bride might conceivably be based on other Biblical passages, like Jer. 2:2; Isa. 62:5, the references to "lily" and "dove" point unmistakably to our book. The only passage in the *Septuagint* which may point to a mystical interpretation is the rendering of *mērōsh 'amānāh* in 4:8 as "from the beginning of faith," but this is far from certain, since *'amānāh* has the meaning "faith" in Neh. 10:1. The Mishnah cites the description of Solomon's wedding in 3:11 and refers it to the giving of the Torah and the building of the Temple.[10] The same view underlies the Targum on the book, and the Midrash *Shir Hashirim Rabbah*, as well as many talmudic interpretations of various verses in the book.

Medieval Jewish commentators like Saadia and Rashi accepted

[7] After the preliminary draft of this study was completed, Professor H. H. Rowley sent me his new book, *The Servant of the Lord and other Essays on the O. T.* (London, 1952). It contains a characteristically thorough yet engrossing study of "The Interpretation of the Song of Songs" (pp. 189–234), incorporating two earlier papers of the author in *JThS*, vol. 38 (1937), pp. 337 ff., and *JRAS* (1938), pp. 251 ff., and supplemented with valuable references to recent literature, from which I have profited greatly. On p. 232, note 3, he cites the older surveys of the history of the interpretation of the *Song*, from C. D. Ginsburg and Salfeld to Vaccari and Kuhl, to which he acknowledges his own indebtedness.

[8] Cf. Hos., chaps. 1–2; Jer. 2:2; 3:1–3; Isa. 50:1 f.; 54:5; 62:4 f.; Ezek., chaps. 16, 23; II Esdras 9:38; 10:25 ff.

[9] In Christian circles, Theodore of Mopsuestia, who opposed its place in the canon, was excommunicated as a heretic.

[10] Cf. M. Ta'an. 4:8.

its assumptions unhesitatingly. It is possible that the unconventional Abraham Ibn Ezra may be expressing his secret doubts on the subject by the method he employs in his commentary, which he divides into three parts, the first giving the meaning of the words, the second the literal meaning of the passage, and the third the allegorical interpretation.[11] Commentators differed as to details, but the general approach was clear. The book narrates, in symbolic fashion, the relationship of God and Israel from the days of the Patriarchs and the Exodus, extols the steadfast love and protection that God has given His beloved, and describes the fluctuations of loyalty and defection which have marked Israel's attitude toward its divine Lover.

When the Christian Church accepted the Hebrew Scriptures as its Old Testament, it was easy to transfer the parable from the old Israel to the New Israel, though there were variations of attitude. The first known allegorical treatment was that of Hippolytus of Rome, written early in the third century. He precedes Origen, Jerome, and Athanasius, who referred the book to Christ and the Church, while Ambrosius and Cornelius a Lapide identified the Shulammite with the Virgin Mary. Other figurative theories also were not lacking. Some of the older commentators, like Origen and Gregory of Nyassa, saw in it an allegory of the mystical union of the believing soul with God, a particularly congenial view, since mysticism has often expressed itself in strongly erotic terms.[12] Luther saw in it an allegory of Christ and the Soul.

The allegorical theory has been generally abandoned by modern scholars in its traditional guise. Yet a few contemporary Roman Catholic scholars[13] and some Orthodox Jewish writers[14] still interpret the book as an allegory of Israel's history.

---

[11] To be sure, in dealing with a similar procedure by Origen in his *Commentary on the Song*, Rowley (*op. cit.*, p. 200) denies that it implies any adherence to a literal meaning of the text. But what may be true of the 3rd century Church Father is not necessarily true of the medieval Jewish commentator, who frequently felt compelled to disguise his adherence to heterodox views, and even to polemize against ideas that he found attractive.

[12] Cf., for example, R. A. Nicholson, *The Mystics of Islam* (London, 1914); G. Scholem, *Major Trends in Jewish Mysticism* (New York, 1946).

[13] Cf. P. Joüon, *Le Cantique des Cantiques* (1909); A. Robert, "Le genre littéraire du Cantique des Cantiques," in *Revue Biblique*, vol. 52 (1943–44), pp. 192 ff.; E. Tobac, "Une page de l'histoire de l'exégèse," in *Revue d'histoire ecclésiastique*, vol. 21, part 1, 1925, pp. 510 ff., reprinted in *Les cinq livres de Salomon* (1926); G. Ricciotti, *Il Cantico dei cantici* (1928).

[14] Cf. J. Carlebach, "Das Hohelied," in *Jeschurun*, vol. 10 (1923), pp. 97 ff., especially pp. 196 ff.; R. Breuer, *Das Lied der Lieder* (1923).

Other forms of the allegorical theory have not been lacking. Isaac Abrabanel and his son Leo Hebraeus, basing themselves on the fact that Wisdom is described in *Hokmah* literature as a beautiful woman, who is contrasted with the "Woman of Folly" in Proverbs,[15] interpreted the beloved in the Song as a typological symbol of Wisdom, a view suggested in modern times by Godek and Kuhn. However, the details in the Song of Songs are both too concrete and too numerous to support this or any other allegorical view, which has accordingly found few adherents.

III. THE CULT THEORY

The most modern form of the allegorical theory regards our book as the translation of a pagan litany. In 1914, O. Neuschatz de Jassy suggested that it is a version of an Egyptian Osiris ritual, while Wittekindt proposed the view that it is a liturgy of the Ishtar cult.[16] The theory was most vigorously propagated by T. J. Meek,[17] who, in 1922, published the theory that the Song is a liturgy of the Adonis-Tammuz cult, the rites of which were undoubtedly practised in Palestine and were denounced by the prophets.[18]

The influence of Mowinckel and others[19] has popularized the view that the poetry of the Old Testament is in large measure cult-material, most of which was taken over from Canaanite religion.[20] Once the

[15] Cf. Prov. 8:1 ff.; 9:1 ff., 22 ff.; B. S. 14:23; 15:2; Wisdom of Solomon 8:2 ff., and see *per contra* Prov. 9:13 ff.

[16] Cf. Neuschatz de Jassy, *Le Cantique des Cantiques et le mythe d'Osiris-Hetep* (1914); Th. J. Meek (see the following note for references); W. Wittekindt, *Das Hohe-Lied und seine Beziehung zum Istarkult* (Hanover, 1925); L. Waterman, in *JBL*, vol. 45 (1936), pp. 171–87; Graham and May, *Culture and Conscience* (1936), pp. 22 f. The same theory underlies the excellent commentary of M. Haller, *Die fünf Megillot* (Tuebingen, 1940).

[17] Cf. his papers, "Canticles and the Tammuz Cult," in *AJSL*, vol. 39 (1922–23), pp. 1 ff.; "The Song of Songs and the Fertility Cult," in W. H. Schoff ed., *The Song of Songs, a Symposium* (Philadelphia, 1924), pp. 48 ff.; "Babylonian Parallels for the Song of Songs," in *JBL*, vol. 43 (1924), pp. 245 ff. In private correspondence he later informed Professor Rowley that he had modified his views, without indicating in what direction. Cf. Rowley, *op. cit.*, p. 213, note 5.

[18] Cf. Isa. 17:10 f.; Ezek. 8:14; Zech. 12:11. On the other hand, it is doubtful whether Jer. 22:18 refers to the ritual, and Isa. 5:1–7 surely is not connected with it.

[19] S. Mowinckel, *Psalmenstudien*, vol. 2 (1922), pp. 19 ff.; Hempel, *Die althebraeische Literatur und ihr hellenistisch-juedisches Nachleben* (Wildpark-Potsdam, 1930–34), pp. 24 ff.; O. Eissfeldt, *Einleitung in das A. T.*, pp. 94 ff.; E. H. Leslie, *The Psalms*, pp. 55–62.

[20] Cf. L. Kohler, *Theologie des A. T.* (Tuebingen, 1936), pp. 169, 182;

theory was set in motion, not merely the Psalms, but also the books of Hosea,[21] Joel,[22] Nahum,[23] Habakkuk[24] and Ruth,[25] have been interpreted, in whole or in part, as liturgies of the fertility-cult, and the end of the process is not yet in sight. Thus Haller declares that the Song of Songs was originally a cult-hymn for the spring festival of Ḥag Hamazzot, which the Canaanites observed with a litany glorifying Astarte as "the beloved" and Baal as Dod "the lover." The Song, we are assured, is part of the widespread Near Eastern ritual of the dying and reviving god.[26] Deuteronomic theologians are then assumed to have profanized the orginally sacred text, so that today it appears as a collection of erotic lyrics of a secular character. The impact of recent archaeological discoveries, particularly of Ugaritic literature, have given this view a new vogue.

Nevertheless, the cult-theory of the book can not be sustained, we believe, when subjected to analysis.[27] It begins with a hypothetical approach to the Hebrew Bible which is highly dubious. That the Old Testament contains only *Kultdichtung* is a modern version of the attitude which regards the Bible exclusively from the theological standpoint, instead of recognizing it, in A. B. Ehrlich's succinct phrase, as the Hebrews' "national literature upon a religious foundation."[28] Undoubtedly the religious consciousness permeated all aspects of the national life in ancient Israel, but the existence of secular motifs can not be ignored, particularly in the area of Wisdom, to which the art of the Song belonged, and with which it was identified.

There are other telling objections to the view that the Song of Songs is a liturgy of the dying and reviving god. That the Ḥag Hamazzot was such a festival in Israel is a gratuitous assumption, with

G. Hoelscher, *Geschichte der israelitischen und juedischen Religion* (Giessen, 1922), pp. 62 ff.

[21] Cf. H. C. May, "The Fertility Cult in Hosea," in *AJSL*, vol. 48 (1930), pp. 73 ff.

[22] Cf. I. Engnell, in *Svenske Biblikst Uppslagsverk*, vol. 1 (1948), col. 1075 f.

[23] Cf. P. Humbert, in *ZATW*, NF, vol. 3 (1926), pp. 266–80; *idem*, in *RHPR*, vol. 12 (1932), pp. 1 ff.

[24] Cf. E. Balla, in *Religion in Geschichte und Gegenwart*, 2nd ed., vol. 2 (1928), col. 1556 f.; E. Sellin, *Einleitung in das A. T.* (7th ed., 1935), p. 119.

[25] Cf. W. E. Staples, in *AJSL*, vol. 53 (1936), pp. 145 ff.

[26] The difficult נִדְגָּלוֹת in 6:4, 10, he regards as a textual error for *Nergal*. On this passage, see *Commentary ad loc.*

[27] Cf. the trenchant criticism of N. Schmidt, "Is Canticles an Adonis Liturgy?", in *JAOS*, vol. 46 (1926), pp. 154–64; and H. H. Rowley, in *JRAS* (1938), pp. 251–76, now amplified in his *The Servant of the Lord*, pp. 219–32.

[28] Cf. his *Kommentar zu Psalmen* (Berlin, 1905), p. V.

no evidence in Biblical or in post-Biblical sources. The proponents of the theory are driven to adduce as proof the synagogue practice of reading the Song of Songs during Passover. The oldest reference to the custom, however, is in the post-Talmudic tractate *Sopherim*, which probably emanates from the sixth century C. E.,[29] at least a millennium after the composition of the book. Its liturgical use at Passover can be explained without recourse to far-fetched theories. It is eminently appropriate to the festival, both in its literal sense and in the allegorical interpretation which has been official for centuries. Its glorification of spring (cf. 2:11 ff.; 7:11 ff.) was congenial to the "festival of Abib" and the Midrash refers many passages in the text to the Exodus, with its moving spirits, Moses and Aaron. Efforts have indeed been made to find vestiges of the Ishtar-cult in the text, but none of them are at all convincing.[30] The Song of Songs makes no references to

[29] Cf. Sopherim 14:16 (ed. Higger, p. 270), which apparently refers to its reading on the *last* two days of the festival, as observed in the Diaspora: בשיר השירים קורין אותו בשני לילי ימים טובים של גלויות האחרונים חציו בלילה אחד וחציו בלילה שני: On the date of the tractate, see Higger, *op. cit.*, Introduction. The reason is indicated in *Maḥzor Vitry*, p. 304: ולכן אנו אומרים בפסח על שם שיר השירים מדבר מנאולת מצרים שנא' לסוסתי ברכבי פרעה וכל העניו מדבר מארבע גלויות למבין: The medieval *piyyutim* which have entered the Passover liturgy are largely based on the *Song of Songs*, as in the cycle of hymns which begin with ברח דודי (Cant. 8:14).

[30] It has been argued that *zāmīr* in 2:12 must mean a "ritual song" (cf. Meek, in Schoff, *op. cit.*, pp. 49 f.). Actually, the root *zāmar* means "sing, make music," generally used in the Bible of ritual song, to be sure, but only because of the Bible's preoccupation with religious themes. The noun is used in a secular sense in Isa. 25:5, זְמִיר עָרִיצִים, "the tyrants' song of triumph"; note the parallelism. See also Isa. 24:16; Job 35:10. It is noteworthy that the Talmud interprets Ps. 119:54, זְמִרוֹת הָיוּ־לִי חֻקֶּיךָ, in a specifically secular sense and criticizes David for treating God's laws as mere song: מפני מה נענש דוד בעווא מפני שקרא לספר תורה זמרות היו לי חקיך "Why was David punished in the incident of Uzzah (II Sam., chap. 6)? Because he called the scroll of the Law mere 'songs' " (B. Sotah 35a; Yalkut Shimeoni, Psalm 119, sec. 480d). Actually, זְמָר is cognate to the noun זָמִיר (cf. קָדִים, קֶדֶם; זָרִים, זָרֶם, Jer. 18:14, on which see Gordis, in *JThS*, vol. 41, 1940, pp. 37 ff.). The root is used to refer to a secular song *in direct connection with our book*; cf. Tos. Sanh. 12:10: רבי עקיבא אומר המנענע קולו בשיר השירים בבית המשתאות ועושה אותו כמין זמר אין לו חלק לעולם הבא "He who gives his voice a flourish in reading the Song of Songs in the banquet-halls and makes it a *secular song* has no share in the world to come."

The 10th century agricultural calendar of Gezer lists ירחו זמר, "two months of vine-pruning." The Vav is best taken as a dual, status construct (so I. G. Février, in *Semitica*, vol. 1, 1948, pp. 33 ff.; W. F. Albright, in J. E. Pritchard, *Ancient Near Eastern Texts*, Princeton, 1950, p. 320a), rather than simply as the old nominative ending (so D. Diringer, *Le iscrizioni anticho-ebraiche Palestinesi*, 1934, p. 5; Th. C. Vriezen-J. H. Hospers, *Palestine Inscriptions*, Leyden, 1951, pp. 12 f.). However, *yrhw zmr* comes after ירחו קץ and therefore, as Dalman (*PEFQS*, 1909, p. 119) points out, "it cannot be the first pruning which comes in March, but the second,

this spring festival or any other, or, for that matter, to any ritual observance.

Proponents of the theory are in diametrical disagreement on a fundamental issue, whether the alleged pagan ritual in the Song has remained in its original and unmodified form[31] or whether it has been drastically reworked as part of the JHVH cult.[32] If the former is the case, it is an insuperable difficulty that the entire book makes no references to dying[33] nor to weeping for the dead god[34] nor to the decay of

in June or July." Rowley (p. 229 f.) follows him in interpreting *Song* 2:12 as a reference to this second pruning. But this is very unlikely, since, according to the poem, the winter and the rain are just over and the first bloom is taking place. For this, June-July is too late. So, too, the parallelism with "the voice of the turtledove" strengthens the view that *zāmīr* refers to "singing." Accordingly, there is no basis for interpreting it either as a ritual song or as meaning "pruning," which is against the parallelism and the context (against Ehrlich).

Another *locus classicus* of the cult-theory has been מַה־דּוֹדֵךְ מִדּוֹד (5:9), which is rendered, "Who but Dod is thy beloved?" (Meek, in Schoff, *op. cit.*, p. 55; Wittekindt, *op. cit.*, p. 82). Meek argues that *mah* means "who" in Babylonian, or that it is a textual error for מִי. But even this assumed correction does not suffice to yield the required sense, which would have been expressed by some such phrase as מִי דּוֹדֵךְ כִּי־אָם דּוֹד; cf. Isa. 42:19, מִי עִוֵּר כִּי אִם־עַבְדִּי, "Who is blind but My servant?" Actually, there is no real evidence for Dod as a divine name used in Israel. Conversely, Meek's objection to the usual interpretation is not valid. He argues that the rendering "What is thy beloved more than another beloved?" requires the addition of "other." I do not know of an exact analogy in Hebrew for the construction, on either view, but supplying "other" is justified. Cf. Gen. 3:1: וְהַנָּחָשׁ הָיָה עָרוּם מִכֹּל חַיַּת הַשָּׂדֶה, "The serpent was wiser than all *other* beasts of the field"; cf. *ibid.* 3:14; 37:3; Deut. 7:7; 33:24, בָּרוּךְ מִבָּנִים אָשֵׁר, "Blessed above all *other* sons is Asher"; Judg. 5:24; Ps. 45:3. The usual rendering, literally, "What is thy beloved above (the class of) lover," is therefore eminently satisfactory.

The difficult כַּנִּרְגָלוֹת (6:4, 10) is emended to כַּנֵרְגַל, "like Nergal," the Babylonian god of the underworld, who was the partner of Ninurta, the summer sun, and "whose powerful gaze is contrasted with the milder light of the dawn and the moon (Haller)." Even if this attractive suggestion be adopted, it offers no real support to the cult-theory. Ritual texts and mythological allusions may employ the same figures, but they are worlds apart in their outlook, as Homer and Milton, or Vergil and Dante, abundantly attest. Biblical writers use Leviathan, Tehom, Mot, Reseph, and other elements of pagan religion, but for them, unlike the Babylonian and Ugaritic epics, these are mythological references, not religious verities. This is particularly true with regard to astronomical phenomena. Cf. the Babylonian names of the months in the Hebrew calendar, which include the god Tammuz himself, or the modern names of the planets, the days of the week and the months. Actually, there are some important objections to the emendation. For these and for an alternative interpretation, see the Commentary *ad loc.*

[31] So de Jassy, *op. cit.*, p. 90.

[32] So Meek, in *Song of Songs — a Symposium*, p. 53.

[33] "Death" and "Sheol" are mentioned in 8:6 purely as similes.

[34] As, e. g., in Ezek. 8:14 ff., where it is clearly condemned as a foreign rite.

nature. If the latter alternative is true, there is the additional problem of a JHVH liturgy in which the Divine name is absent, either explicitly or as an allusion.

It is human love, not that of a god, which is glorified in the Song, and that with a wealth of detail, which rules out an allegorical interpretation. The entire book deals with concrete situations, whether of love's repining, or its satisfaction, of lovers' flirtations, estrangement and reunion. Moreover, the frequent references to specific localities in the topography of Palestine effectively rule out the likelihood that this material could have been used for liturgical purposes. For the essence of a liturgy is that it is typological, being concerned with a generalized and recurrent pattern of activity.[35]

One is, of course, at liberty to assume that our book represents a secular reworking of a no longer extant litany of an assumed Israelite cult which has left no record of its existence behind it. Such a complex of unsubstantiated hypotheses recalls the argument that the ancient Hebrews must have known of wireless telegraphy, because archaeologists in Palestine have found no wires in their excavations.

Neither the older nor the more recent allegorical interpretations of the Song of Songs are convincing explanations of the original character of the book. In favor of the traditional Jewish and Christian allegories is the fact that they have their own independent charm, which the cult-theory does not possess.

It may even be granted, as Rowley well says, that "we, for our profit, may rightly find in the images of the Song, as in all experience, analogies of things spiritual," but that "does not mean that it was written for this purpose and that the author had any such idea in mind."[36] The key to the book must be sought in a literal interpretation of the text, as the surest basis for true understanding and lasting appreciation of its greatness.

IV. The Literal Interpretation

While the allegorical view of the Song of Songs early became official, it is noteworthy that the Rabbis were well aware that in many circles it was being interpreted literally. That the allegorical view had difficulty in winning universal acceptance is clear from the warmth

---

[35] This consideration disproves the hypothesis that Psalm 2 is part of a liturgy of enthronement. The historical background is clearly that of a revolt of subordinate rulers, much too specific a situation for a recurrent litany of royal enthronement.

[36] Op. cit., p. 201.

of the statement in the Tosefta:[37] "He who trills his voice in the chanting of Song of Songs and treats it as a secular song, has no share in the world to come."

Obviously, too, the literal view of the book lay at the basis of the doubts expressed in the Mishnah as to its canonicity:[38] "The Song of Songs and Koheleth defile the hands (i. e. are canonical). Rabbi Judah says, The Song of Songs defiles the hands, but Koheleth is in dispute. Rabbi Jose says, Koheleth does not defile the hands and the Song of Songs is in dispute. . . . Rabbi Simeon ben Azzai said, I have a tradition from the seventy-two elders on the day that Rabbi Eleazar ben Azariah was appointed president of the Academy that both the Song of Songs and Koheleth defile the hands. Said Rabbi Akiba, Heaven forfend! No one in Israel ever disputed that the Song of Songs defiles the hands. For all the world is not as worthy as the day on which the Song of Songs was given to Israel, for all the writings are holy, but the Song of Songs is the Holy of Holies. If they differed at all, it was only about Koheleth. Rabbi Johanan ben Joshua, the brother-in-law of Rabbi Akiba, said, Both the division of opinion and the final decision accorded with the statement of Ben Azzai, i. e. they differed on both books and finally decided that both were canonical."

Nevertheless, the literal view, which was rejected on the conscious level, won a measure of unconscious acceptance even in Rabbinic circles. That the book deals with human love is implied in the well-known statement: "Solomon wrote three books, Proverbs, Koheleth, and the Song of Songs. Which did he write first? . . . Rabbi Hiyya the Great said, He wrote Proverbs first, then the Song of Songs, and then Koheleth. . . . Rabbi Jonathan said, The Song of Songs he wrote first; then came Proverbs, and then Koheleth. Rabbi Jonathan proved it from normal human behavior. When a man is young, he sings songs. When he becomes an adult, he utters practical proverbs. When he becomes old, he voices the vanity of things."[39]

---

[37] Cf. Tos. Sanh. 12:10. The text is quoted in note 30 above.

[38] Cf. Mishnah 'Eduy. 5:3; Tos. Yad. 2:14. In M. Yad. 3:5, the final decision in its favor is registered: שיר השירים וקהלת מטמאין את הידים ר' יהודה אומר שיר השירים
מטמא את הידים וקהלת מחלוקת ר' יוסי אומר קהלת אינו מטמא את הידים ושיר השירים מחלוקת
ר' שמעון אומר קהלת מקולי בית שמאי ומחומרי בית הלל אמר ר' שמעון בן עזאי מקובל אני מפי שבעים
ושנים זקנים ביום שהושיבו את ר' אלעזר בן עזריה בישיבה ששיר השירים וקהלת מטמאין את הידים אמר
רבי עקיבא חס ושלום לא נחלק אדם מישראל על שיר השירים שלא תטמא את הידים שאין כל העולם
כולו כדאי כיום שניתן בו שיר השירים לישראל שכל הכתובים קודש ושיר השירים קודש קדשים ואם
נחלקו לא נחלקו אלא על קהלת אמר ר' יוחנן בן יהושע בן חמיו של ר' עקיבא כדברי בן עזai כך
נחלקו וכך גמרו:

[39] Midrash Shir Hashirim Rabba 1:1, sec. 10. רבי יונתן אומר שיר השירים כתב תחילה

In the Christian Church, too, the literal view was known and fought. The position of the fourth-century Theodore of Mopsuestia was declared a heresy by the Second Council of Constantinople in 353. His objections to the book were repeated, in 1544, by Chateillon, who wanted it expunged from the canon as immoral. It is characteristic of the broader conception of canonicity in Judaism that no such demand for its elimination was made, even by the anonymous French Jewish commentator of the twelfth century or by a few other medieval Jewish writers who regarded it as a song written by Solomon for his favorite wife.[40] In the sixteenth and seventeenth centuries various scholars suggested that the book was a collection of eclogues, and analogies with the Idylls of Theocritus were frequently invoked. It was Herder who, in 1778, explained it as a collection of songs extolling the joys of human love. This view, however, receded in popularity for over a century thereafter.

V. The Dramatic Theory

In the eighteenth century, years before Herder, several scholars, like Wachtel (1722) and Jacobi (1771), espoused the view that the book is a drama. This view is perhaps foreshadowed by two Greek manuscripts of the fourth and fifth centuries C. E., which actually supply speakers for the various verses of the book. It is the dramatic theory which was the first to win wide acceptance among modern scholars and readers in two variant forms. According to the first, adopted by Delitzsch, there are two main characters, King Solomon and a rustic Shulammite maiden, and the book consists substantially of expressions of love by the two principal characters. According to the other view, first propounded by J. S. Jacobi and elaborated by Ewald, there are three characters, a beautiful maiden, her shepherd lover, and King Solomon, who on a visit to the countryside discovers her and becomes enamored of her beauty. The luxuries of the royal court and the blandishments of the king are powerless to shake her love. At length the young rustic lovers are reunited, and the play ends with a song on the lips of the maiden and her shepherd lover.[41]

ואחר כך משלי ואח״כ קהלת ומייתי ליה ר' יונתן מדרך ארץ כשאדם נער אומר דברי שיר הגדיל אומר
דברי משלות הזקין אומר דברי הבלים:

[40] Cf. Rowley, p. 206, n. 4.

[41] The division of the book according to both views is conveniently set forth by S. R. Driver, *Introduction to the Literature of the O. T.* (New York, 1906), 12th ed., pp. 437–43.

It is obvious that the second view has a dramatic tension lacking in the first, and it has been increasingly espoused by those who favor the dramatic theory.[42]

Nonetheless, the theory suffers from several grave drawbacks which must be clarified, since this view is still taken for granted in most popular treatments of the book:

1. That speakers must be supplied for the various lines would be natural and constitutes no difficulty. The crux lies in the fact that *the entire plot must be read into the book and the natural intent of the words be ignored again and again.* One or two instances must suffice. Thus Driver, following Ewald, attributes the opening section, 1:2–7, to the maiden in these words:

> "Scene I. (The Shulammite and Ladies of the Court.) — The Shulammite, longing for the caresses of her absent shepherd-lover, complains that she is detained in the royal palace against her will, and inquires eagerly where he may be found."

Now none of this reconstruction is in the actual text. The opening verses 2–4 make no reference to the lover as being absent. Moreover, the complaint in verse 7, which is addressed directly to him, is not that she is detained against her will by the king, but that she can not find him among his fellow-shepherds. Finally, this interpretation does not do justice to the text of verses 5 and 6. The proud words of these verses, in which the maiden praises her own beauty and explains her dark hue, are hardly the words appropriate to one who wants to flee the court and the king's advances, in order to be reunited with her shepherd lover.

The remainder of chapter 1 is assigned to Scene II as follows:

> Solomon (9–11) seeks to win the Shulammite's love. The Shulammite (12, aside) parries the king's compliments with reminiscences of her absent lover.— Solomon (15) — The Shulammite (v. 16, aside) takes no notice of the king's remark in v. 15 and applies the figures suggested by it to her shepherd-lover.

Now verses 9–11 might *conceivably* be Solomon's words as he seeks to win her love, but there the plausibility of the reconstruction ends. Verse 12, "while the king sat at his table (or couch), my spikenard

---

[42] Thus only the older commentators, Hengsterberg, Keil, and Kingsbury, favor the first. The second is accepted by Driver (*op. cit.*). The catena of commentators who share this view is given in R. H. Pfeiffer, *Introduction to the O. T.* (New York, 1941), p. 715.

sent forth its fragrance" (JV), can not naturally mean (*pace* Driver)
that "while the king *was away from me*, at table with his guests, my
love (for another) was active" (italics Driver's). Nor is there anything
to suggest that vv. 13–14 *parry* any of the king's compliments or
that she has more than one lover in mind at all. Finally, assigning
v. 15 to the king and v. 16 to the maiden, who is *referring to her absent
lover*, means to divide what is obviously a single literary unit, both in
form and in content. The love-dialogue is clear:

"Thou art fair, my beloved, thou art fair, thine eyes are doves."
"Thou art comely, my lover, and sweet, and our couch is
fragrant."

There are many other instances where the exigencies of the dramatic theory artificially divide obvious literary units. Thus 2:2 is
assigned to Solomon, while 2:3 is again attributed to the maiden as
an *aside*.

2. Incidents which in a drama should have been acted out are nar-
rated, as in 2:8; 5:1, 4. This is perfectly comprehensible in a lyric,
but not in a play.

3. The climax of the plot is assumed to be 8:11 ff. Here the young
lovers spurn the luxury of Solomon's court in favor of the delights of
love, contrasting the high financial returns of Solomon's vineyard
with the "vineyard" of the beloved's person and charm. But precisely
here the dramatic form is totally lacking. Solomon is not addressed
at all, which is what one should have expected in a dramatic confronta-
tion of king and commoner as they contend for the maiden's hand.
Instead, it is clear from the narrative phrase, "Solomon had a vineyard at Baal-Hamon," that Solomon is *not* present, and the adjuration
in v. 12 is therefore rhetorical and not actual.

4. The distribution of the name "Solomon" in the book is worthy
of note. Aside from the superscription (1:1), the name occurs six
times more — in 1:5, where it is used generically,[43] and in two other
sections, i. e. in chapter 3 (vv. 7, 9, 11) and in chapter 8 (vv. 11, 12),
and *nowhere else*. The full significance of this fact will be discussed
below. Suffice it to note that if Solomon were a principal protagonist
of the drama, we should expect a more consistent use of his name

---

[43] יְרִיעוֹת שְׁלֹמֹה means "Solomonic curtains," being parallel to "Arab tents,"
like our phrases "Louis Quatorze furniture," "Queen Anne fashions," and the like.
On the meaning and poetic structure, see the Commentary *ad loc.*, and see Gordis,
"Al Mibneh Hashirah Haivrit Haqedummah," in *Sefer Hashanah Liyhudei Amerikah*
(New York, 1944), pp. 151 ff.

throughout the book than the existing pattern. As for the noun "king," *hammelek*, which might conceivably be an epithet for Solomon in the drama, it is also very rare in the book, occurring in only three additional passages (1:4, 12; 7:6) besides its use together with "Solomon" in two cases (3:9, 11).

5. That the book is a drama presupposes that it is a literary unit. This is, however, ruled out categorically by linguistic considerations. The noun *pardēs* (4:13) is of Persian origin, and the passage in which it occurs can not, therefore, be older than the Persian period (6th century B. C. E.). On the other hand, in 6:4 the lover compares his beloved to Tirzah and Jerusalem. The parallelism makes it clear that the poet must be referring to Tirzah, the old capital of the Northern Kingdom of Israel, which was replaced with Samaria by Omri in the first half of the ninth century B. C. E.[44] A lover does not usually praise his beloved by comparing her to a city ruined centuries earlier! Hence this passage can not be later than the ninth century B. C. E.[45] It is obvious that if at least one passage in a book can not be earlier than the sixth century, and another can not be later than the ninth, the work is manifestly not a literary unit, and the dramatic theory is conclusively ruled out.

VI. SONG AS A BRANCH OF WISDOM

In the Hebrew Bible, the Song of Songs finds its place in the third section, the Hagiographa, in proximity to Psalms and Lamentations on the one hand, and to Proverbs and Job on the other. This third section is not a heterogeneous collection but, on the contrary, possesses an underlying unity, being the repository of *Hokmah* or Wisdom. Wisdom was much more than a branch of literature. It included all the technical arts and practical skills of civilization. The architect and the craftsman, the weaver and the goldsmith, the sailor and the magician, the skillful general and the wise administrator of the state, are all described as *hakāmīm*, "wise."[46] In Rabbinic Hebrew the epithet *hakāmāh* is applied also to the midwife.[47]

---

[44] Cf. I Kings 16:23 f. Oesterley-Robinson, *History of Israel* (Oxford, 1932), p. 463, dates the accession of Omri to the throne as 886 B. C. E. W. F. Albright, in L. Finkelstein, ed., *The Jews* (New York, 1949), p. 33, places it as circa 876 B. C. E.

[45] The grounds for maintaining that there is even older material in the book, going back to the 10th century B. C. E., will be presented below.

[46] Cf. Gen. 41:8; Ex. 28:3; 35:25, 31; 36:1; Isa. 10:13; 29:14; 44:25; Jer. 9:16; 10:9; 49:7; Ezek. 27:8; Ps. 107:27.

[47] Cf. M. Shab. 18:3; M. R. H. 2:5; B. 'Er. 45a.

While all these phases of *Hokmah* disappeared with the destruction of the material substratum of ancient Hebrew life, it was these practical and technical aspects of *Hokmah* that were primary, and its more theoretical meaning to designate metaphysical and ethical truths embodied in literature is a later development. This semantic process from the concrete to the abstract, which is universal in language, is validated also for the Greek *sophia*, which is strikingly parallel in its significance.[48] The basic meaning of the Greek word is "cleverness and skill in handicraft and art," then "skill in matters of common life, sound judgment, practical and political wisdom," and ultimately, "learning, wisdom and philosophy."[49] The adjective *sophos* bears the same meanings, being used of sculptors and even of hedgers and ditchers, but "mostly of poets and musicians."[50] The noun *sophistes*, "master of a craft or art," is used in the extant literature of a diviner, a cook, a statesman, and again of poets and musicians. From Plato's time onward, it is common in the meaning of a professional teacher of the arts.[51]

The Hellenic culture-area serves as a valuable parallel, shedding light not only on the origin and scope of ancient "Wisdom," but also on the development and function of the teachers and protagonists of the discipline, but that is not our concern here.[52]

One of the most frequent uses of the term *Hokmah* refers it to the arts of poetry and song, both vocal and instrumental, for the composition and the rendering of songs, which were often done by the same individual, required a high order of skill. Thus the women skilled in lamentation at funerals are called *hakāmōth* by Jeremiah (9:16).

---

[48] Cf. Gordis, *KMW*, pp. 18 ff., 30 ff., for a full discussion of the parallels between Greek *sophia* and Hebrew *Hokmah*.

[49] In its first meaning, *sophia* is applied to Hephaestus, the god of fire and the arts, to Athena, to Daedalus, the craftsman and artist, and to the Telchines, a primitive tribe who are represented under three aspects: 1) as cultivators of the soil and ministers of the gods; 2) as sorcerers and envious demons, who had the power to bring on hail, rain, and snow, and to destroy animals and plants; and 3) as artists working in brass and iron. (Gen. 4:20–22 offers a suggestive parallel.) *Sophia* is used of such crafts as carpentry, driving a chariot, medicine and surgery. It is used preeminently of singing, music and poetry (*Homeric Hymn to Mercury*, lines 483, 511; Pindar, *Odes*, 1, 187; Xenophon, *Anabasis*, 1, 2, 8). On the usage of all three terms here discussed, cf. Liddell-Scott, *Greek Lexicon*, s. v.

[50] Pindar, *Odes*, 1, 15; Euripides, *Iphigenia in Tauris*, 12:38; Plato, *Laws*, 696c. See Liddell-Scott, *op. cit.*, s. v.

[51] Pindar, 1, 5, 36; Aeschylus, *Fragmenta*, 320; cf. Liddell-Scott, *op. cit.*, s. v.

[52] For a characterization of Wisdom, see Gordis, "The Social Background of Wisdom Literature," in *HUCA*, vol. 18 (1944); *KMW*, pp. 16–38.

The relationship between Wisdom and Song was so close that the terms were used interchangeably. Thus in I Kings 5:10–12 we read: "And Solomon's wisdom excelled the wisdom of all the children of the east, and all the wisdom of Egypt. For he was wiser than all men: than Ethan the Ezrahite, and Heman, and Calcol, and Darda, the sons of Mahol; and his fame was in all the nations round about. And he spoke three thousand proverbs; and his songs were a thousand and five."[53] Ethan and Heman, who are here described as "wise,"[54] are the eponymous heads of the musical guilds in the Temple in Jerusalem. Note, too, that the same Biblical passage attributes both "proverbs" and "songs" to Solomon.

The songs of the prophet Balaam are called $m\bar{a}sh\bar{a}l$ (literally, "parable, proverb"), perhaps because the poems are replete with comparisons (Num. 23:7, 18; 24:3, 15, 20, 21, 23). But essentially the term is a synonym for "song." Thus the unknown poets, whose military epic is cited in the fragment in Num. 21:27–30, are called $m\bar{o}shel\bar{i}m$ (literally, "makers of $mashal$"). The term $h\bar{i}d\bar{a}h$, "riddle, mysterious saying," together with $m\bar{a}sh\bar{a}l$, is applied to the song played on the $kinn\bar{o}r$, "the lyre" (Ps. 49:5; 78:2). The recently discovered evidence from Ugaritic sources corroborates the Biblical tradition, previously dismissed as anachronistic, which declares that these guilds of singers are very ancient. In fact, they probably go back to the Canaanite period.[55]

Now Wisdom literature as a whole began on a secular note and only gradually took on a religious coloration. This is clear from the chronology of the best attested branch of Oriental Wisdom, that of Egypt, where religious motifs are late in appearing. Similarly in Israel, as Pfeiffer correctly says, "We know positively that the secular school (of Wisdom) flourished before the pious."[56] The oldest popular Hebrew proverbs and the Wisdom fragments imbedded in the Historical books are all secular in character.[56a]

A similar development may be postulated for that branch of Wisdom called $shir$, which includes both poetry and music. The Song certainly played an important role in religious ritual, at sacrifices processions and festivals, but it was not limited to these areas. Actu-

[53] Or, "five thousand," with the Septuagint.

[54] Cf. I Kings 5:10–12 with I Chron. 15:19 and the superscriptions of Psalms 88 and 89, and see Gordis, KMW, p. 17.

[55] So W. F. Albright, in an unpublished paper, "The Canaanite Origin of Israelite Musical Guilds."

[56] Cf. Pfeiffer, $op. cit.$, p. 650.

[56a] Cf. I Sam. 10:12; 24:14; II Sam. 14:14; I Kings 20:11; II Kings 14:9; Jer. 23:28; 31:29; Ezek. 16:44; 18:2.

ally, it was coextensive with life itself, dealing with all the normal secular concerns of life, such as combat and victory,[57] the opening of a well, vintage and harvest,[58] feasting and carousing,[59] the glory of nature and the tragedy of death.[60]

Undoubtedly the poems of national significance, like those of war and victory, were given a religious character, as in the "Song of the Sea" (Ex. 15) or the "Song of Deborah" (Judg. 5), since the historical experience of Israel was conceived as reflecting the will of God. But it is noteworthy that many of the briefer snatches of song which are preserved in prose narratives and are explicitly quoted from older collections, like the *Book of the Wars of the Lord* (Num. 21:14) and the *Book of Jashar* (probably the "Book of Heroes," Josh. 10:13; II Sam. 1:18; I Kings 8:53 in the Greek), are purely secular in content. The Song, like Wisdom, as a whole, later developed a religious stamp, but it remained an acquired characteristic.

For self-evident reasons, the secular note would be more likely to be preserved in the area of love and courtship, which has inspired more poetry and music than any other field of human interest. Into this area, where the sensual and the physical play so important a part, the traditional religious coloration would have the greatest difficulty in penetrating. The existence of secular love-songs in ancient Egyptian and Akkadian literature,[61] as well as among contemporary Arab peasants and city dwellers,[62] strengthens this contention, besides offering many a key to the understanding of the Biblical song.[63]

VII. THE SONG OF SONGS AS A COLLECTION

If the Song of Songs be approached without any preconceptions, it reveals itself as a collection of lyrics. This view of the book was taken by a Middle High German version of the 15th century, which

---

[57] Cf. Gen. 4:23; Judg. 15:16; I Sam. 18:7.

[58] Cf. Num. 21:17 ff.; Isa. 16:10; 22:13; 27:2.

[59] Cf. Amos 6:5; Isa. 5:12; Job 21:12; Ps. 69:13.

[60] II Sam. 1:19 ff.; 3:33; cf. Amos 5:16; Jer. 9:16 (מקוננות, חכמות, יודעי נהי).

[61] Cf. A. Erman, *Literature of the Ancient Egyptians*, tr. by Blackman (London, 1927); J. B. Pritchard, *Ancient Near-Eastern Texts Relating to the O. T.* (Princeton, 1950).

[62] For a collection of these songs, containing text, translation, and notes, see the extremely valuable study of St. H. Stephan, *Modern Palestinian Parallels to the Song of Songs* (Jerusalem, 1926).

[63] Cf. Gordis, *KMW*, pp. 16 ff., and note R. H. Pfeiffer's judicious statement on the subject (*Introduction*, p. 712): "There must have existed in Palestine during the last centuries of our era a considerable amount of erotic poetry of which our book alone survives by accident."

divided it into 54 songs. A long catena of modern scholars have adopted the same position, though naturally differing on the division of the book.[64]

A great step forward in the interpretation of the Song was taken in 1893, when J. G. Wetzstein, Prussian consul in Damascus, called attention to the nuptial customs of the Syrian peasants, who have the couple sit on a "throne" during the wedding-meal as "king" and "queen," while the guests sing songs of praise (wasf), glorifying the bride and groom. In some cases, the bride also executes a "sword dance" during the festivities. The affinities with several passages in the Song are obvious, and many scholars were accordingly led to interpret the entire collection as emanating from such wedding celebrations.[65]

That the praise of the bride on her wedding day was a regular feature of Jewish weddings in Second Temple days, and that these songs of praise were a technical art and therefore part of Hokmah, is clear from an ancient Talmudic tradition. It reads as follows: "How is one to dance before (i. e. praise) the bride? The Shammaites declare: 'By praising her for the qualities she actually possesses.' The Hillelites say: 'By saying of every one, O bride, beautiful and gracious.' "[66] The same function continued to be performed by the badḥān or humorous rhymster at East-European weddings until our day.

On the other hand, it is clear that some of the lyrics in the Song of Songs are not connected with wedding ceremonies or with married love at all.[67] The only justifiable conclusion is that the Song of Songs,

---

[64] Jastrow and Budde each finds 23 songs, though they differ on the subdivisions. Haller finds 26, Bettan 18. We divide the book into 28 songs, several of which are fragmentary and some of which may be doublets. Popular songs frequently circulate in many versions.

[65] So Wetzstein, Budde, Stade, Cornill, Kautzsch, Jastrow, Cassuto, Goodspeed, and others. Cf. Pfeiffer, op. cit., p. 716.

[66] B. Ket. 16b: כיצד מרקדין לפני הכלה בית שמאי אומרים כלה כמות שהיא בית הלל אומרים כלה נאה וחסודה.

[67] At the same time, Gebhardt's objection to the view in toto is much too extreme. The doubts which have been raised by H. Granquist as to the existence of such a custom as a "king's week" among the Arabs of Palestine overlook the clear-cut references in Jewish practice to שבעת ימי המשתה, "the seven days of feasting" following the wedding, which are observed to the present day with a repetition of the Seven Nuptial Blessings first recited at the marriage. Moreover, Rothstein's objection that the bride is never called "queen" in the Song loses part of its force when it is recalled that while Rabbinic literature cites and elaborates on the proverb חתן דומה למלך, "The bridegroom may be compared to a king" (Pirke de Rabbi Eliezer, chap. 16), there is no corresponding phrase about the bride. However, the Sabbath is described

like the Psalter, is an anthology, running a wide gamut of its emotions. It contains songs of love's yearning and its consummation, of coquetry and passion, of separation and union, of courtship and marriage.

The division of the songs will depend upon the changes in theme, viewpoint, background or form. These criteria will not always be sufficiently exact to command universal assent. Much will be dependent upon the literary taste and insight, as well as upon the knowledge, of the interpreter. But this is simply a restatement of the truth that exegesis is essentially an art, which rests upon a foundation of scientific knowledge.

VIII. SOLOMON IN THE SONG OF SONGS

If the Song of Songs is an anthology of love poems, how are the seven instances of Solomon's name in the text to be explained? For on this view he is neither the author of the book, as the traditional view claims, nor its hero, as is maintained by the dramatic theory.

Several of these instances are easy to explain. In the opening verse of the book (1:1), we have a later superscription by an editor who had already accepted the theory of Solomon's authorship.[68] In three other passages, the use of the name is authentic. These are in 1:5 ("Solomonic hangings"), where it is a descriptive term like our "Louis XIV furniture," and in 8:11 and 12, where Solomon is used to typify a possessor of great wealth, as the ancients used "Croesus" or as moderns might use the name of a multi-millionaire like Vanderbilt or Rockefeller.

The other three examples of Solomon's name, it is generally suggested, are glosses which were induced by these authentic occurrences of the name in the text, and were reinforced by the tradition of Solomon as the "great lover" (I Kings 11:1 ff.). It would therefore be natural to believe that he was also intended by the word *melekh*, "king," in the Song, though the word actually referred to the bridegroom. Hence "Solomon" was added as a gloss in three more verses (3:7, 9 and 11).

For all its apparent plausibility, however, this approach is not adequate. Not only do we find "Solomon" used without the word "king" in 3:7, but the word "king" occurs several times in the book without the gloss "Solomon" (1:4, 12; 7:6). The clue to the solution

as both "queen" and "bride" in Talmudic and post-Talmudic sources; cf. Shab. 119a and Solomon Alkabetz' famous hymn *Lechah Dodi*.

[68] Hence the use of the relative *še*, instead of *'asher*, and the high valuation on the book expressed in the title. See the Commentary *ad loc*.

lies in the observation that the only three passages in the book in which Solomon is apparently unauthentic (3:7, 9, 11) *all occur in the same poem*.

This poem (3:6–11) is generally regarded as a rustic wedding song. But if it is scrutinized carefully, a variety of problems arise:

The poem contains many descriptive traits which, literally viewed, can not apply to a simple peasant wedding. The pillars of smoke (v. 6) and the sixty heroes trained in war (v. 7) are often dismissed as poetic hyperbole. However, v. 10, "he made its pillars of silver, the top thereof of gold, its seat of purple, its inside being inlaid with ivory,"[69] is much too explicit to be merely the product of a poet's heightened imagination. A country lover might describe the open fields as his fresh couch, the cedars as the walls of his home and the sycamores as his rafters (1:16 f.), but the circumstantial description of a luxurious palanquin, far beyond the reach of a rustic couple, would be a mockery rather than a tribute of praise to the lovers.

Another difficulty is the explicit national note to be found only here. Not only do we have a reference to "the daughters of Jerusalem" (3:10), which is familiar from other passages in the Song (2:7; 3:5; 5:8, 16; 8:4), but "the daughters of Zion" (3:11) are mentioned in this poem, and nowhere else. Most important of all, while the Palestinian locale pervades the entire book, the only national reference, that to "Israel," occurs in 3:7.

Moreover, the occurrence of Solomon's name in these verses is not easily solved by deletion. In 3:7, "king" does not occur and "Solomon" can not be removed without leaving a lacuna. Hence the entire stich must be dropped. In v. 11 the deletion of "Solomon" irreparably destroys the rhythm of the verse.[70] Even in v. 9, the excision of the name is not required on rhythmic grounds.[71]

---

[69] Reading הָבְנִים with Graetz and most moderns, or הַבִּים with Tur-Sinai; cf. I Kings 10:22; Amos 6:4. See the Commentary.

[70] The meter of the verse is 2:2:2 ‖ 3:3:3:. *B'yōm hᵃthunāthō* receives three beats, both because of its length and the exigencies of the meter. On this procedure, as well as on the technique of longer stichs at the end of a poem, cf. the study by Gordis cited in note 43 above, pp. 136–59, especially pp. 140 f., 145 f.

[71] The *kinah* rhythm is not limited to the 3:2 pattern, its basic trait being a longer stich followed by a shorter. Scholars have been led astray here by the conjunctive accents linking *hammelekh šelōmōh*, when actually the words belong to separate stichs, with a 4:3 meter for the verse, which is in climactic or complementary parallelism. Similarly, in Num. 23:7 the words *bālāq melekh mō'ābh*, though linked by conjunctive accents, belong to separate stichs. For a full discussion of the meter of the verse, cf. Gordis, "A Wedding Song for Solomon," in *JBL*, vol. 63 (1944), especially pp. 266 ff.

These difficulties, cumulatively viewed, all point to the conclusion that we have here no song for a rustic wedding but, quite the contrary, an epithalamium for a wedding of great luxury, one possessing even national significance. In fact, all the details cited are easily explained by one assumption — *that we have here a song composed on the occasion of one of Solomon's marriages to a foreign princess*, probably an Egyptian.[72]

Such a poem has survived in Psalm 45, in which an Israelite king is marrying a Phoenician princess.[73] Obviously, songs were composed for and sung at different stages of the wedding ceremony. Psalm 45 is addressed to the king (vv. 3–10) and to his new queen (vv. 11–14), perhaps after the marriage rites had been concluded. Our song, on the contrary, is a chorus of welcome addressed to the bride as her procession approaches from across the wilderness which separates Palestine on the east and on the southwest from its neighbors.

All the details of the poem are explained naturally on this simple premise. The princess travels with a large retinue, which encamps at night and sends up pillars of smoke (v. 6). Her palanquin was sent to her by Solomon and is escorted by the royal bodyguard, sixty of the heroes of Israel (v. 7; cf. II Sam. 23:8 ff.; I Kings 1:10). The litter is made of the finest cedarwood of Lebanon, one of the by-products of his commercial relations with Phoenicia. Its decorations of silver, gold, purple and ivory (v. 10) are in keeping with Solomon's penchant for luxury, and may well have been prepared by the noble ladies of Jerusalem (v. 11).

All the references to Solomon in the book, aside from the title, are thus authentic, including the three references in this song, which dates from Solomon's reign. The presence of this poem, in the collection, would serve as the nucleus for the tradition attributing the entire book to Solomon.

In connection with this early date for the song, two linguistic problems must be considered. Graetz derived the word *'apiriōn*, "litter, couch" (3:9), from the Greek *phoreion*, which would imply a

---

[72] On Solomon's foreign marriages in general, cf. I Kings 11:1 ff.; on his marriage to the Egyptian princess, cf. I Kings 3:1.

[73] The dating of Psalm 45 has been the subject of wide difference of opinion. While it has been referred to Solomon (Kirkpatrick), to Jehu (Briggs, ICC), to Ahab and Jezebel (Hitzig, Buttenwieser), or to Jehoram and Athaliah (Delitzsch), Pfeiffer's judgment that the king's name can not now be determined is the soundest view. Evidently, such compositions must have been common, though only one has survived in the Psalter. The preservation of another example in the *Song of Songs* is perfectly natural, in fact even more appropriate.

period considerably after Solomon's day. However, this etymology is far from certain. On independent grounds, many scholars prefer other derivations, the most plausible being from the Sanskrit *paryanka*, "sedan, palanquin."[74] That Solomon had regular commercial relations with India is being increasingly recognized, as scholars re-evaluate the Biblical evidence in the light of new extra-Biblical data.[75] Ac-

[74] So Robertson-Smith in Yule, *Glossary of Anglo-Indian Words*, p. 502; Brown-Driver-Briggs, *Lexicon*, s. v. Tur-Sinai (in his paper, p. 4, n. 1) adduces an Akkadian parallel *ap* (*p*)*aru*, meaning "hut of reeds" and also "head covering." Erbt and Wittekindt read '*appidyōn*, from Babylonian '*aphad* = "come as messenger." Zapletal reads *appadan*, Babylonian "tent," which occurs in Dan. 11:45. Tur-Sinai makes a new suggestion in *Halashon Vehasepher* (Jerusalem, 1951), p. 389, where he argues that a litter is too small an object and suggests that the word is actually a scribal combination of אף, "also," and an unknown word רידן.

[75] The technical term "ship of Tarshish," which the book of Kings applies both to Solomon's vessel that sailed with Hiram's navy and brought back "gold, silver, ivory, apes and peacocks" (I Kings 10:22) and to the ships of Jehoshaphat which sailed from the southern port of Ezion-geber (I Kings 22:49), has been regarded as a generic term for a large vessel, no matter what its destination, like our English "Indiaman." Thus it could be used of vessels going eastward to Arabia, Africa, or even India. This, in spite of the fact that the place-name "Tarshish" has been generally equated with some port west of Palestine, such as Carthage (LXX on Ezek. 27:12), the Roman province of Africa (Targum on I Kings 22:49; Jer. 10:9), Tarsus in Cilicia (Josephus, *Antiquities*, 1, vi, 9), Etruscan Italy (Cheyne), Tharsis on the Black Sea (Desnoyers), Tharros in Sardinia (Covey-Crump), or, as is most generally accepted, Tartessos in Spain (first proposed by Eusebius and revived by Bochart; cf. W. Max Müller, *Dictionary of the Bible*, vol. 4, pp. 683 f.; Galling, *Biblisches Reallexikon*, pp. 510 f.).

On the other hand, it seems clear that the book of Chronicles thought of Tarshish as lying to the east of Palestine, since it uses the phrase "ships going to Tarshish" in its account of these same nautical enterprises of Solomon and Jehoshaphat (II Chron. 9:21; 20:36). This was long dismissed as another example of the unreliability of the Chronicler. Recent scholarship has, however, gone far in rehabilitating his credibility (cf., for example, Von Rad, *Die Geschichtsbildung der Chronistischen Werke*, Stuttgart, 1930; Martin Noth, *Ueberlieferungsgeschichtliche Studien*, Halle, 1943; W. F. Albright, *From the Stone Age to Christianity*, Baltimore, 1940, p. 268). It is, therefore, not impossible that the Chronicler's view of Tarshish is another example where his value was unduly discounted in the past. Thus Bochart's old attempt to validate the Chronicler's references by assuming that there were two localities referred to as "Tarshish," one in the Western Mediterranean, the other in the Indian Ocean, was dismissed summarily by scholars (cf. W. Max Müller, *Dictionary of the Bible*, vol. 4, p. 684n). On the other hand, J. Hornell recently contended vigorously that Tarshish refers to "a great mart on the west coast of India," from which gold, spices, pearls, and other gems were shipped westward (cf. his paper, "Naval Activity in the Days of Solomon and Rameses III," in *Antiquity*, vol. 21, p. 72). This view is favorably considered by Salo W. Baron (*A Social and Religious History of the Jews*, 2nd ed., New York, 1952, vol. 1, p. 321, n. 3.).

Whatever the identification of Tarshish, the Oriental provenance of '*apiriōn*,

cording to our sources (I Kings 10:22), Solomon's imports from the East included ivory, apes ($q\bar{o}ph$) and peacocks ($t\bar{u}k\bar{\imath}$). As the derivation of these words indicates (Sanskrit, $kapi$; Malabar, $toqai$, $toqhai$), India was the point of origin of these luxuries. In addition, Solomon's ships might well have imported the palanquin, or at least the materials from which it was constructed, from India, together with its native name.

The syntactic construction in 3:7 ($mi\underline{t}\underline{t}\bar{a}th\bar{o}$ $\check{s}elli\check{s}^el\bar{o}m\bar{o}$), which would seem to reflect Aramaic influence,[76] does not represent an insuperable objection to a Solomonic dating for the poem as a whole. Popular songs often tend to be supplemented and modified with time, so that a late phrase may enter an early poem, and inconsistencies result. The composite character of folk-poetry must always be kept in mind. Thus, in a modern Palestinian love-lyric, the girl Fulla is addressed as Jewish, Mohammedan and Christian, all in the course of the eleven stanzas of the song.[77] While she is called Serena, a popular name of Spanish-Jewish actresses (stanza 4), she is described as making her ablutions before prayers, a Mohammedan practice (stanza 6), while the marriage ceremony is described by a specifically Christian term (stanza 9).

Moreover, the evidence is constantly growing that an "Aramaic" usage is not necessarily late in Hebrew. Not only in Northern Israel, but even in the south, the close linguistic affinities of the two languages[78] were strengthened by continuous relations between Israel

---

rather than the proposed Greek etymology for the word, becomes increasingly more plausible.

[76] Cf. Dan. 3:26; 4:23, and such frequent Mishnaic locutions as רבונו של עולם.

[77] Cf. Stephan op. cit., pp. 35 f.

and Syria throughout the pre-Exilic period.[79] The usage may, accordingly, be older than can at present be documented in our extant sources.[80]

Moreover, related instances of pronominal anticipation occur in Biblical Hebrew and Phoenician.[81] Hence we are not forced to delete the entire clause from the poem, or even to assume that it was introduced later.[82]

Whatever approach be adopted on this detail, the unique features of this poem mark it as a royal wedding-song going back to Solomon's reign. It is at present the oldest datable unit in the book. By contributing to the growth of the tradition of Solomonic authorship, it helped to win inclusion for the entire Song of Songs in the canon of Scripture.

IX. DATE OF THE BOOK

Being lyrical in character, with no historical allusions, most of the songs are undatable. There are, however, a few exceptions, which have already been noted. The song in which Tirzah, the early capital of North Israel, is referred to (6:4), must predate the year 876 B. C. E., when Omri made Samaria the capital of his kingdom, while the use of a Persian word like $pard\bar{e}s$ (4:13) can hardly antedate the 6th century. Yet even this latter inference must be qualified by the consideration already adduced above, that folk songs often undergo many

cf. Isa. 3:5; *Rahab* the mythological monster mentioned in Isa. 30:7; Job 9:13, etc.); Lamed accusative (2:15; 8:13; cf. Lev. 19:18, 34; II Sam. 3:30).

Authentic Aramaic borrowings seem to be חרכים (2:9); כתל (2:9); סתו (2:11); סמדר (2:13, 15; 7:13); פג (2:13); מנף (5:3); סנסנים (7:9); and סוגה (7:3), though new texts may change the picture. See note 80.

[79] Cf. A. T. Olmstead, *A History of Palestine and Syria* (New York, 1931).

[80] Thus the word *'aśiaḥ* occurs only in the Hebrew of Ben Sira (6:2) with no Biblical parallel, but it is found in the late Aramaic of the...

changes with time, so that later words and expressions may well be inserted into such older material. The grounds for attributing one song (3:6–11) to the period of Solomon have already been set forth. Thus the datable material in the Song spans five centuries. The period begins with Solomon's accession to the throne (c. 960 B. C. E.), includes the early days of the Northern Kingdom (c. 920–876), and reaches down to the Persian era (6th–5th century).

The variations in language, which point to a considerable difference in the dates of the different songs, are only one factor, though decisive, in making it impossible to agree with Rowley, who has "the impression of a single hand" in the Song with "a corresponding unity of theme and style."[83] So, too, the varying geographical locales, from the Lebanon mountains in the north to the Dead Sea region in the south, from Transjordan to the central valleys, plainly point to a different provenance for the various songs. The change from rustic simplicity in some lyrics to the sophistication of the city in others points in the same direction.

It is most probable that the other songs in the book fall within the same four centuries as the datable units, with the bulk of the material being pre-Exilic rather than post-Exilic. The freshness of the poetry, the naturalness of the references to the Palestinian landscape, and the unabashed attitude toward love all seem to point to the period before the Babylonian Exile. No national disaster has yet cast its shadow over the temper of the people, and there is no echo as yet of the deepening of the religious consciousness which followed the Restoration under Cyrus and the reforms of Ezra and Nehemiah. That most of the place-names are northern and eastern also points to the pre-Exilic era, in fact to the period preceding the destruction of the Northern Kingdom in 722 B. C. E., since the Jewish settlements were restricted largely to Judah in the south during the Persian and pre-Maccabean period. The book was redacted in the Persian period, the heyday of Wisdom literature, not later than the fifth century.

X. HEBREW ELEMENTS IN THE SONG OF SONGS

Love lyrics are, as we have seen, difficult to date because their basic emotion knows no limit of time. Since the sentiment is not limited in space, love songs are not specifically national. In this respect, the Song of Songs shares the qualities of Wisdom literature as a whole, which is the most secular and least particularist element of Hebrew literature.

[83] *Op. cit.*, pp. 212 f.

Nonetheless, some specific *national* coloring is to be found in the book. The reference to "the heroes of Israel" (3:7) is needed in this epithalamium of a foreign princess to indicate the nationality of her bodyguard. The "tower of David" upon which the shields of the heroes are hung (4:4) testifies to the widespread living character of the tradition of David's band of heroes, which is now embodied in the lists in II Sam. 23:8 ff.

The only other national notes are *geographical*, the cities, hills, and valleys of the country. Principally, the book reflects the background of Northern Israel. It is the northern mountain range which appears in Hermon and Senir (modern Jebel esh-Sheikh) as well as in Lebanon (now Jebel Libnan) and 'Amana (the modern Jebel Zebedâni).[84] The central territory of Northern Israel appears in Shunem,[85] in Carmel and Sharon, as well as in Tirzah, if its location is to be sought at Tel-el-Fâr'ah. Transjordan appears in Ḥeshbon (modern Hesban), in the south, in the districts of Gilead, and possibly in Bashan to the north.[86] On the other hand, the territory of Judah is sparsely represented. Aside from the references to the daughters of Zion (3:11) and of Jerusalem (3:5; 5:8), only En-gedi on the Dead Sea is mentioned (1:14).

The preponderantly northern coloring of the book, as already noted, is significant in strengthening the view that the songs are predominantly pre-Exilic. The northern provenance of the songs also explains the Aramaisms in the book, which reflect the close proximity of the pre-Exilic Kingdom of Israel to Syria. Foreign products and articles bear foreign names, whether Sanskrit or Persian.[87]

Attention to the geographical locale is sometimes helpful in delineating the literary unit. The passage 1:9–17 is often regarded by commentators as one song.[88] However, the references to Pharaoh's horses and chariots (v. 9), which were most likely to be seen in Southern Palestine, and the mention of the vineyards of En-gedi on

---

[84] On the modern identification of these sites, see Wright-Filson, *Historical Atlas to the Bible* (Philadelphia, 1945), pp. 107 ff. While Deut. 3:9 informs us that Senir was the Amorite equivalent for Hermon, the Song (4:8) treats them either as distinct mountain peaks or as a wider designation for the Anti-Lebanon range.

[85] The equivalence of "Shulammite" with "Shunemite," long maintained, is attested by *Sulem*, the modern Arabic name of *Shunem*. On other recent theories, see the Commentary *ad loc.*

[86] If כְּמִגְדַּל הַשֵּׁן in 7:5 is to be read as הַבָּשָׁן, in view of the other geographical similes in the *waṣf*.

[87] Thus פַּרְדֵּס (4:13) is not a garden, but a park. Of the spices mentioned, אֲהָלוֹת, קִנָּמוֹן and כֹּפֶר are probably Indian, like אַרְגָּמָן and אַפִּרְיוֹן. אֱגוֹז may be Persian. See the Lexicons of Brown-Driver-Briggs and Baumgarten-Kohler, *s. v.*

[88] So e. g., Jastrow, Haller. Pfeiffer (*op. cit.*, p. 710) regards vv. 12–17 as a unit.

the western shore of the Dead Sea (v. 14), point to Judah in the south. On the other hand, the reference to the lovers' meeting in the forest, their "house walled with cedars" (v. 17), must necessarily reflect a North Israelite locale, since cedars never grew in southern Palestine.[89] So, too, the Aramaized form $ber\bar{o}th\bar{\imath}m$, "sycamores," for the more common Hebrew $ber\bar{o}\check{s}\bar{\imath}m$ (v. 17), points to the Northern Kingdom, which was more exposed to Aramaic influence. It is therefore clear that the passage consists of two independent songs (1:9–14 and vv. 15–17).

When this is recognized, other divergences which tended to be overlooked or misunderstood receive a natural and unforced explanation. The first song speaks of the beloved as luxuriously decked out in jewels (vv. 9–11), and the lover is called "king" (v. 12) and is therefore the bridegroom. He is probably speaking during the festivities of the bridal week and hence uses the plural ($na'aseh$, v. 11) in the presence of his friends. Hence, too, the frank reference to sexual intimacy (vv. 12–13). The second song, on the other hand, reflects the simplicity of an outdoor tryst of lovers (note $d\bar{o}d$, v. 16), not of the bride and groom, hence the delicate reticence regarding their relationship.

Religious motifs are even rarer in the book than specific national references. In the noun $\check{s}alhebhethy\bar{a}h$, "flame of God" (8:6), the Divine name is used to express the superlative, and the word is equivalent in meaning to "a mighty flame." This usage has many analogies in Biblical Hebrew.[90]

We believe that Hebrew religious attitudes, hitherto unrecognized, lie at the base of a unique phenomenon in the book, the adjuration "by the gazelles and the hinds of the field" (2:7; 3:5), "not to disturb love until it be sated." That the gazelle and the hind were symbolic of love is, of course, clear from Biblical and post-Biblical Hebrew, where they were used as metaphors for a graceful and loving young woman.[91] Ebeling, in his study of Babylonian magic, calls attention to the Babylonian practice of tying a gazelle to the head of the bed and a ram at the foot as a magical rite to induce potency, with the formula, "like that ram may my husband love me."[92]

---

[89] Cf. *Enzyklopedia Miqrait* (Jerusalem, 1950), vol. 1, p. 554b.

[90] Cf. מַאְפֵּלְיָה, "deep gloom" (Jer. 2:31); מֶרְחַבְיָה, "great enlargement" (Ps. 118:5); גִּבּוֹר צַיִד לִפְנֵי ה׳, "an exceedingly mighty hunter" (Gen. 10:9); אַרְזֵי אֵל, "mighty cedars" (Ps. 80:11).

[91] Cf. אַיֶּלֶת אֲהָבִים וְיַעֲלַת חֵן (Prov. 5:19). These and similar terms are frequent in the love poetry of Jehudah Halevi, Immanuel of Rome, and other medieval Hebrew poets.

[92] Cf. J. Ebeling, "Liebeszauber im alten Orient," in *Mittheilungen der altorientalischen Gesellschaft*, I (1905), pp. 27, 33.

This is, however, far removed from an oath "by the gazelle," particularly for the strongly monotheistic Hebrews. A closer parallel is afforded by the Greek custom, practiced by no less a figure than Socrates, of swearing by an animal, as e. g. "by the dog," "by the goose," or by any nearby plant or object, such as "by the caperberry," "by the almond" and "by the cabbage."[93] The Greek philosophers defended this usage by asserting that the Greeks never intended to swear by the animals as gods, but used the animals as substitutes for gods. This was no mere apologetics, but a reflection of the widespread fear of the consequence of an unfulfilled oath. Hence arose the desire for an "escape formula."

Another factor, however, often enters into the choice of a substitute, which has been overlooked — *a similarly sounding term, even if irrelevant or virtually meaningless, is often chosen.* Thus the Rabbinic vow-term *korbān* would frequently be replaced by *kōnām*.[94] In contemporary colloquial English, this phenomenon can be clearly observed. "Gosh darn" does duty for "God damn," "Gee," for "Jesus," "Jiminy Crickets" for "Jesus Christ," "Holy Cow" for "Holy Christ," etc.[95] Older substitutions of the same kind that entered English literature are "zounds" for "By God's wounds," "Marry" meaning "indeed," for "By Mary," "Dear me," probably for "Dio Mio," "By Cripes" for "By Christ." The German replaces "Gott" by "Potz" in *"Potzwelt," "Potzwetter"* and *"Pottsblitz."* The Frenchman changes "Dieu" into *bleu* in "Corbleu," "Morbleu," "Sambleu," and avoids the name of God altogether by swearing by "nom de nom."

Of the common speech of the Hebrew populace, little, if any, has reached us, and so the only extant example of this phenomenon is to be found in our book.

The most solemn Hebrew adjuration would be *be'lōhei ṣebhā'ōth* or *be'ēl šaddai*, "by the Lord of Hosts" or "by the Almighty."[96] The

---

[93] Cf. the discussion in S. Lieberman, *Greek in Jewish Palestine* (New York, 1942), pp. 125–27, who cites some of the abundant material assembled in P. Meinhardt, *De forma et usu iuramentorum*, pp. 77 ff., and Hirzel, *Der Eid*, p. 96, note 2.

[94] Cf. Lieberman, *op. cit.*, p. 129, note 106.

[95] Cf. Burgess Johnson, *The Lost Art of Profanity* (New York, 1948); esp. pp. 26, 101, 116, 117. I am indebted to Professor Mario A. Pei for this reference. I was unable to consult *A Dictionary of Profanity and Its Substitutions* by M. R. Walter, on deposit in manuscript form in the Princeton University Library, to which Johnson refers.

[96] The most popular oaths naturally invoked the God of Israel: a) חי ה', "As JHVH liveth" (I Sam. 14:39, 45; 19:6, and often; I Kings 1:29; 2:24, and often; Jer. 4:2; 5:2, and often; Ruth 3:13); (אלהים) נשבע בה' (Josh. 2:12; 9:19; I Kings 1:17; 2:8, etc.). b) חי האלהים (II Sam. 2:27); נשבע באלהים (Gen. 21:23). c) (rarely)

deepseated reluctance to use the Divine name, which finds expression in the Third Commandment (Ex. 20:7), became increasingly felt with time. This tendency is mirrored in such Biblical books as Esther and Ecclesiastes, as well as in the editing of Psalms, and finds varied expression in Rabbinic literature.[96a] The desire to avoid mentioning God's name would be particularly strongly felt in connection with an oath concerned with the physical aspects of love. Hence, the lover replaces such customary oaths as $bē'lohei\ ṣ^ebhā'ōth$ or $b^e'ēl\ šaddai$ by a similarly sounding phrase $biṣ^ebhā'ōth\ 'ō\ b^e'ay^elōth\ hassādeh$, "by the gazelles or the hinds of the field," choosing animals, which symbolize love, for the substitutions. It is likely that the Septuagint retained some recognition of the oath by rendering the unique Hebrew phrase "in (or, by) the powers and the forces of the field."[97] The Midrash also recognized the irregular character of the oath in the Song and identified "the gazelles and the hinds" with "the hosts of heaven and earth."[98] Here, as elsewhere, the homily rests upon a fine perception of the essential meaning of the text.

חי אל (Job 27:2). d) חי ה' אלהיך (I Kings 17:12; 18:10); נשבע לה' (Zeph. 1:5; Ps. 132:2).

Additional solemnity undoubtedly attached to oaths with more elaborate formulas as a) חי ה' אלהי ישראל (I Sam. 25:34; I Kings 17:11); b) חי ה' צבאות, "As JHVH, Lord of Hosts, liveth" (I Kings 18:15; II Kings 3:14); ונשבעות לה' צבאות (Isa. 19:18). A possible double oath occurs in only one poetic passage: חי ה' וברוך צורי, "God liveth and my Rock is blessed" (II Sam. 22:47 = Ps. 18:47). So also the oath בְּחֵי הָעֹולָם, "By Him who liveth eternally" (Dan. 12:7).

To avoid mentioning JHVH, oaths by His name became common: בשם ה' (Isa. 48:1); בשמו (Deut. 6:13; Jer. 12:16); בשמי הגדול (Jer. 44:26); בשמי (Jer. 12:16).

Joint oaths invoking God and a human being also occur: a) חי ה' וחי נפשך, "As God lives and as does your soul" (I Sam. 20:3; 25:26; II Kings 2:2; 4:30); b) חי ה' וחי אדני המלך, "As God lives and as does my lord, the king" (II Sam. 15:21).

The Lord Himself swears by His own being: a) חי אני, "As I live" (Num. 14:21; Jer. 22:24; Ezek. 5:11; 14:16, and often; Zeph. 2:9). b) חי אנכי (Deut. 32:40); בי, "By Myself" (Gen. 22:16; Isa. 45:23; Jer. 22:5; 49:13). c) בקדש, "By His holiness" (Amos 4:2); בקדשי, "By My holiness" (Ps. 89:36). d) בנפשו, "By His essence, literally, soul" (Jer. 51:14; Amos 6:8). e) בימינו, "By His right hand" (Isa. 62:8). f) בגאון יעקב, "By the glory of Jacob," an epithet for God (Amos 8:7).

[96a] Cf. now the illuminating study by S. S. Cohon, "The Name of God, a Study in Rabbinic Theology," in *HUCA*, vol. 23, 1950–51, Part I, pp. 579–604.

[97] Reading ἐν ταῖς δυνάμεσι καὶ ἐν ταῖς ἰσχύσεσι τοῦ ἀγροῦ. Cf. Siegfried *ad loc.*

[98] Cf. Midrash Shir Hashirim Rab. 2:7: במה השביען ר' אליעזר אומר השביען בשמים ובארץ. בצבאות בצבא של מעלה ובצבא של מטה: "By what did he (*sic*) adjure them? R. Eliezer says, 'He adjured them by heaven and earth. *Biṣ^ebhā'ōth* means by the host (*ṣ^ebā'*) above and by the host below.' "

In this reticence with regard to the use of the Divine name, particularly in the context of sensual love, as well as in its pervasive delicacy of expression, which will be discussed below, the Song reveals itself as authentically within the Jewish tradition.

At times, the differences between the Hebrew poet and his Oriental confrères prove highly revealing of the Hebrew *ethos*. Moreover, what the Song does not say is often as significant for its Israelite outlook as any overt Hebrew element.

Thus, hunting was a favorite sport in Egypt and Mesopotamia, as literary sources and archaeological discoveries abundantly indicate.[99] In a love-song emanating from "the Golden Age" of Egyptian lyric poetry in the 18th dynasty,[100] the maiden expresses the yearning for her lover:

> "How good it would be,
> If thou wert with me
> When I set the trap."

She is referring to a small trap set for bird-catching. It is noteworthy that in all the references to nature in the Song, hunting is not mentioned. Nimrod and Esau were hunters, but the taking of animal life for sport was not popular in ancient Israel,[101] an attitude crystallized further in Rabbinic Judaism.[102]

Even more characteristic of the Hebrew spirit is the absence of the personification of nature in the Song. In the Egyptian poem "The Tree in the Garden" the poet goes on to say, "The tree speaketh."[103] For the Hebrew poet, nature serves as the glorious background for human love, but never as more, exactly as nature is the manifestation of the creative power of God for the Psalmist and for Job.[104]

The age-old relationship of wine, women, and song finds its reflection, of course, in the Song, for wine-drinking was widespread in Israel. Nonetheless, references in our book to the first member of

[99] Cf. K. Galling, *Biblisches Reallexikon* (Tuebingen, 1937), pp. 286 ff.

[100] Cf. J. A. Wilson, in Pritchard, *op. cit.*, p. 468a.

[101] Cf. W. H. Bennett, in Hastings, *Dictionary of the Bible*, vol. 2, pp. 437 f.; K. Galling, *Biblisches Reallexikon* (Tuebingen, 1937), pp. 286 ff. On the other hand, killing animals in self-defense was naturally practised (cf., for example, Judg. 14:6; I Sam. 17:34 ff.), and some game animals were used for food (Deut. 12:15, 22; I Kings 5:3).

[102] The Jewish laws of *shehitah*, which prescribed slaughter with a knife, effectively ruled out the use of birds or animals killed in the hunt.

[103] Cf. Erman, *op. cit.*, p. 249.

[104] Cf., *inter alia*, Psalms 19 and 105; Job, chaps. 38–41.

the triad are very few.[105] Nothing is to be found resembling these lines of an Egyptian love song:[106]

"Her lover sitteth at her right hand,
The feast is disordered with drunkenness."

The absence of this theme in the Song may, of course, be the result of the choice of poems in the collection. It is at least equally likely that it reflects a negative attitude toward drunkenness, which became traditional in Judaism.

Another common aspect of love-poetry, virtually missing here, is the motif of faithlessness and jealousy.[107] On the other hand, the Egyptian maiden complains:[108]

"What meaneth it that thou wrongest another heart and me?"

To be sure, coquetry and the maiden's resistance to the lover's advances occur as themes,[109] but no "love triangle" is to be met with in our book. This absence, however, must be accidental, or the result of the editor's choice — the human emotion involved is ubiquitous and must have existed in ancient Israel.

XI. Extra-Hebrew Parallels to the Book

The universality of love as an emotion and an experience, which is responsible for the absence of any considerable degree of specific Hebrew coloration in the book, should make us wary about postulating direct borrowings from other peoples in these songs. Mere resemblances of theme are not sufficient. What is methodologically required is a special sequence of theme or some other unusual feature, not explicable in terms of Hebrew background. A few centuries later, the Palestinian city of Gedara was the home of the gifted Greek poets Meleager and Menippus the Epicurean, was described in the 1st

gift was limited to the Greek inhabitants of the country and that the Hebrews were congenitally incapable of love-poetry.

With the all but universal rejection of a Greek date for the book today, scholars have turned instead to the Egyptian culture-milieu in seeking evidence of borrowing in the Song of Songs. Thus, it has been argued that the use of '$\bar{a}h\bar{o}th$, "sister," for "beloved" is an Egyptian usage. Being unhebraic, the word was glossed by $kall\bar{a}h$, "bride," everywhere except in the last passage (4:9, 10, 12; 5:1, 2).[110] Actually, the assumption of glossing is not supported by the meter. Of the five passages where the term occurs, it is not accompanied by $kall\bar{a}h$ in one (5:2), and it can not be a gloss in two others (4:9, 12), because its deletion would destroy the rhythm of the text.[111] In the other two passages (4:10; 5:1), metric considerations can not be invoked at all, since either the retention or the deletion of '$\bar{a}h\bar{o}th$ would produce an acceptable rhythmic pattern.[112]

The entire assumption that the usage is unhebraic, however, is unjustified. The Hebrew nouns $r\bar{e}'a$ and $ra'y\bar{a}h$ ($r^{e'}\bar{u}th$), which are common in the meanings "friend" and "neighbor," also signify "beloved."[113] Similarly, the synonyms '$\bar{a}h$ and '$\bar{a}h\bar{o}th$, "brother, sister," develop the parallel meanings of "friend, neighbor" and "beloved."[114] $Ah\bar{o}th$ therefore means "beloved" in the Song, when the lover, in an outburst of emotion, heaps up terms of endearment, coupling "sister"

[110] Cf. Pfeiffer, op. cit., p. 711. As a matter of fact, '$\bar{a}h\bar{o}th$ occurs in the meaning of "beloved" with no gloss, in another song, 8:8. See Commentary ad loc.

[111] The MT in 4:9 has a 3:3:3 meter. The deletion of כַּלָּה would create 2:3:3, a rare, if not impossible, pattern, since as a rule closing stichs are longer than the opening ones only at the end of a literary unit, for the purpose of creating a strong close. See the following note for an example, and cf. the study cited in note 43, p. 146. In 4:12, the rhythm is 3:2:2 which would also be destroyed by omitting כַּלָּה . . .

either with "bride" or with "friend."[115] So too, the Hebrew and Arabic word for "daughter," *bat, bint*, means "girl" and is not restricted to the specific family relationship.[116]

Nor is there any objective ground for assuming that the feeling for nature was an exclusively Egyptian trait. The God speeches in Job manifest a loving insight into nature unparalleled elsewhere, and the prophets and psalmists disclose a love and observation of the external world which needed no foreign influence or literary borrowing.[117]

Of direct borrowings in the authentic sense, there is no evidence. Nonetheless, since love is the same anywhere, the reactions and forms of expression of love-lyrics everywhere will resemble each other. Accordingly, Oriental love poetry, ancient and modern, often sheds light upon the background of the Hebrew poem. Because of the close relationship of love to magic and religion[118] which modern psychology and anthropology have revealed, ancient incantation texts also add considerably to our understanding of the Song.[119]

Tur-Sinai[120] has called attention to the background underlying 8:9:

> If she be a wall,
> We will build upon her a turret of silver;
> And if she be a door,
> We will enclose her with boards of cedar.

---

[115] On the equivalence of אָח and רֵעַ, cf. Ps. 35:14, כְּרֵעַ כְּאָח־לִי הִתְהַלָּכְתִּי; Job 30:29, אָח הָיִיתִי לְתַנִּים וְרֵעַ לִבְנוֹת יַעֲנָה.

[116] Tur-Sinai calls attention to this fact, *op. cit.*, p. 367. This usage is not restricted to Biblical Hebrew (Gen. 30:13; Isa. 32:9; Prov. 31:29), but is common in modern Israeli Hebrew as well.

[117] Cf., on the appreciation of beauty in the Bible, the eloquent presentation of S. Goldman, *The Book of Books*, vol. 1 (New York, 1948).

[118] Cf., *inter alia*, J. G. Frazer, *The Golden Bough* (New York, 1922); A. E. Crawley, *The Mystic Rose* (New York, 1927); B. Z. Goldberg, *The Sacred Fire* (New York, 1930).

[119] Cf. J. Ebeling, "Liebeszauber im alten Orient," in *Mittheilungen der altorientalischen Gesellschaft*, vol. 1 (1925); *idem*, "Aus dem Tagewerk eines assyrischen Zauberpriesters," in *MAOG*, vol. 5 (1931). It is the merit of N. H. Tur-Sinai, in his paper "Shir Hashirim," now reprinted in his *Halashon Vehasepher*, vol. II (Jerusalem, 5711), pp. 351–88, to have utilized this material for the interpretation of our book with great brilliance. At times, however, his deductions, like his basic view of the *Song* as part of a gigantic prose-poetic history of Israel (cf. p. 388), do not carry conviction.

[120] *Op. cit.*, p. 367. We are, however, unable to accept his interpretation (p. 368) that *šeyᵉdubbar bāh* (8:8) means "when incantations are pronounced upon her."

Charms warding off all types of perils were couched in this form. Thus, for example, the Assyrian charm against a crying baby was as follows:

It it is a dog, let them cut off morsels for him!
If it is a bird, let them throw clods of earth upon him!
If it is a naughty human child, let them adjure him with
the oath of Anu and Antu!

Even more apposite, because it demonstrates that $homah$, "wall," and $deleth$, "door," "bar," in 8:9 are synonymous and not antithetic, is the following charm against an enemy:[121]

If he is a door, I will open thy mouth,
If he is a bar, I will open thy tongue.[122]

Obviously there is no incantation implied any longer in the Song, but the formula has survived as a love motif.

While several $wasfs$ in praise of the beloved occur in the book, only one waṣf praising the lover is to be met with (5:10–16). In part the description is highly extravagant and goes beyond the limits of metaphor. Thus, for example, 5:11, 14, 15:

"His head is fine gold . . . .
His hands are rods of gold, set with topaz . . . .
His thighs are pillars of marble
Set upon sockets of gold . . . .

Perhaps these phrases are more than mere poetic hyperbole. This is suggested by a Babylonian adjuration for the recovery of a sick person from illness:[123]

Like lapis lazuli I want to cleanse his body,
Like marble his features should shine,
Like pure silver, like red gold,
I want to make clean what is dull.

The Biblical waṣf may therefore be extolling the health and potency of the lover.

A long-standing difficulty in the Song is presented by 5:1. The first four stichs of the verse speak of the lover enjoying the myrrh,

---

[121]Ebeling, "Aus dem Tagewerk," p. 19.

[122] Ebeling's rendering "seine Zunge" is a $lapsus\ calami$. The Akkadian is $lisânaka$.

[123] $Ibid.$, p. 37.

honey, wine and milk that symbolize the delights of love. The fifth stich of the verse is couched in the plural:

$$'ikh^elu\ r\bar{e}'\bar{\imath}m\ \check{s}^ethu\ v^e\check{s}ikh^er\bar{u}\ d\bar{o}d\bar{\imath}m$$

"Eat, friends, drink abundantly, O loved ones." It is, of course, inconceivable that either the love-struck youth or the maiden would invite others to enjoy the same pleasures as the loved one, and the stich has therefore been emended either to the masculine singular[124] or to the feminine,[125] either procedure requiring no less than five changes. Some have regarded the stich as a misplaced fragment of an independent song.[126] A solution to the problem through an illuminating parallel is offered by an Arab song, widely known all over Palestine and Syria, which would indicate that the poet may address the individual lover in the plural, as well as in the singular:

> Examine me,
> O physician,
> As to what I suffered
> On behalf of the beloved one.

> By God, O Lord!
> This is a wondrous thing;
> Yet my heart melted
> For the beloved ones.[127]

The Hebrew text of 5:1 is therefore in order and the stich is in place.

---

[124] Ehrlich reads: אֱכֹל רֵעִי שְׁתֵה וּשְׁכַר דּוֹדִי.
[125] Haller reads: אִכְלִי רַעְיָתִי שְׁתִי וְשִׁכְרִי דּוֹדִים.
[126] So Budde, who deletes the stich entirely, also Jastrow.
[127] Cf. Stephan, *op. cit.*, p. 80. The text reads as follows:

> *Ykšif 'alayya*
> *Ya tabîb*
> *'Ala-lli atâni*
> *Min il-ḥabîb*
> *Wàllah ya râbb*
> *ha-l-àmru 'ajîb*
> *Wàna 'albi dâb*
> *'Ala l-aḥbâb.*

Stephan (note 3) suggests that the plural *aḥ-bâb* is used for the sake of the rhyme (with *dâb*). That is hardly a compelling reason, since the singular *ḥabîb* would be an excellent rhyme for *'ajîb*, and the second and fourth lines of the stanza would be in rhyme, exactly as in the preceding stanza, *ḥabîb* rhymes with *tabîb*.

XII. MOTIFS AND PATTERNS IN THE COLLECTION

Because of the degree of subjective judgment which must enter into the delimitation of the songs, unanimity is not to be expected. Our own study of the book indicates that it contains twenty-eight songs and fragments, which fall into several patterns, though they often overlap. To mark each basic theme, we have added descriptive titles:

A. SONGS OF YEARNING

The Call to Love (1:2–4)
The Rustic Maiden (1:5–6)
Tell Me Where My Love (1:7–8)
Love's Proud Proclamation (2:4–7)
Would Thou Wert My Brother (8:1–4)
Let Me Hear Thy Voice (8:13–14)[128]

B. SONGS OF FULFILLMENT

Love's Barriers — a Duet (4:12 to 5:1)
How Delightful Is Love (7:7–10)
The Beloved's Promise (7:11–14)[129]
Love Under the Apple-Tree — a Duet (8:5)
Surrender (2:16–17)

C. SONGS IN PRAISE OF THE BELOVED

Bedecked in Charm — a Duet (1:9–14)
My Beloved Is Perfect (4:1–7)
Love's Enchantment (4:9–11)
The Power of Beauty (6:4–7)
The One and Only (6:8–9)

---

[128] V. 14 is best taken as a quotation of the words which the lover wishes to hear (הַשְׁמִיעִנִי: בְּרַח דּוֹדִי), an invitation to enjoy the delights of love (so Haller; slightly differently Bettan).

[129] The entire passage 7:7–10 and 11–14 may constitute a single song in duet form, the first portion being spoken by the lover, the second by his beloved. However, there is no direct plea to the beloved in 7–10, which is essentially a poem of praise, and vv. 11–14 do not constitute a direct answer. We therefore prefer to regard these passages as two independent poems.

D. DUETS OF MUTUAL PRAISE

Our Walls Are Cedars (1:15–17)
Who Is Like My Love (2:1–3)
The Lover's Welcome (2:14–15)

E. LOVE IN THE WORLD OF NATURE

The Time of Singing Is Come (2:8–13)
Call From the Mountains (4:8)
Love's Dawning (6:10–12)[130]

F. DREAM SONGS

The Dream of the Lost Lover (3:1–5)
Love's Trial and Triumph (5:2 to 6:3); see below.

G. THE GREATNESS OF LOVE

The Seal of Love (8:6–7)
The Finest Vineyard (8:11–12)

H. SONGS OF COURTSHIP AND MARRIAGE

A Wedding Song for Solomon (3:6–11)
The Maiden's Dance (7:1–6)[131]
The Ramparts of Love (8:8–10)

I. LOVE'S SORROWS AND JOYS

Love's Trial and Triumph (5:2 to 6:3)

This, the most elaborate and perhaps the most beautiful song in the collection, is a blending of several patterns: (a) the *dream motif* (5:2), which incorporates the themes of coquetry (5:3) and longing (5:4 ff.); (b) the *wasf* in praise of the lover (5:10 ff.); and (c) praise of the delights of love (6:2 f.).

---

[130] It is possible that these verses may be independent fragments. V. 12 is completely untranslatable in its present form. See the Commentary for some of the emendations proposed.

[131] That this is a dance is clear from the fact that the description of the bride begins with her feet. That the occasion is a wedding is highly probable, both from the frank description of her physical charms, by far the most outspoken in the book, and from the reference to the "king," i. e. the bridegroom, in v. 6.

In several instances, the units seem very short and we have merely fragments,[132] perhaps only titles of songs, which are no longer extant in their full form. On the other hand, it must always be remembered that in these charming lyrics we lack the music to which they were invariably sung. The number of words and lines required for a song would therefore generally be fewer than in the case of poetry designed to be read. One has only to compare the few words in the popular Israeli song or traditional Hasidic melody with the longer texts of modern poetry in Hebrew or any other language to see the difference. The longest lyric in the book (5:2 to 6:3), which consists of eighteen verses, is, as has been noted, a highly complex blending of several literary motifs.

In a collection such as this, it is to be expected that phrases and verses will reappear more than once.[133] Glosses are, of course, not to be ruled out *a priori*, but deciding which words are secondary is a particularly precarious undertaking in a collection of popular folk-songs, where additions are natural.[134] Thus the two dream-songs (3:1-5 and 5:2 ff.) repeat the theme of the city watchmen, but the second passage introduces a variation, which is in thorough keeping with the more elaborate development of the song as a whole.

XIII. SYMBOLISM AND ESTHETICS IN THE SONG

It is of the essence of poetry that it employ *symbolism* to express nuances beyond the power of exact definition. This is particularly true of love poetry, where the reticences imposed by social convention add both urgency and piquancy to the use of symbols. Hence the beloved will be compared to a flower (2:1 f.), and the lover to a tree (2:3). The delights of love will be described as fruit (2:3), wine (1:4;

---

[132] Cf., for example, 8:5 or 8:13 f. Albright has made the suggestion that Psalm 68 may contain the titles of a collection instead of being the text of a single poem.

[133] Such are the three adjurations of the daughters of Jerusalem (2:7; 3:5; 8:4), the first two of which include the reference to the hinds and the gazelles of the field. So, too, the same text is repeated in 2:5 and 8:3; the phrase seems less relevant in the second passage. The two dream songs (3:1-5 and 5:2 ff.) repeat the theme of the city watchmen (3:3; 5:7) with a variation in the latter.

[134] Cf. Pfeiffer, *op. cit.*, p. 710, for a list of alleged glosses. Some are essential to the text and need only to be interpreted correctly (as e. g. 5:6). Most rest upon considerations of meter which of themselves do not suffice to justify excisions in the text. Not only is there great uncertainty concerning all theories of Biblical meter proposed (cf. W. H. Cobb, *A Criticism of Systems of Hebrew Meter*, Oxford, 1905), but our lack of the accompanying music makes it impossible to tell what words were repeated or lengthened in the chanting of the songs.

5:1), or perfume (5:1), as milk and honey (5:1), as a garden (4:12; 5:1; 6:2), or a vineyard (8:12). The maiden's resistance to the lover's advances will lead to the metaphor of a sealed fountain (4:12) or a high wall (8:9),[135] and the beloved "enemy" will be attacked with the power of charms (8:8 ff.). The invitation to the lover will be couched in the form of a call to enjoy the vineyard (2:15), the fountain (4:15), or the garden (4:16), while the confession that love's demands have been met will be expressed by the figure of a vineyard unguarded (1:6) or of a gazelle upon the mountains of spices (2:17; 8:14).

Symbolism is much more profound than allegory. In allegory, the imaginary figures that are chosen as equivalents for the real characters and objects involved have no independent reality of their own. The language of symbolism, on the other hand, is superior to literal speech as well, because its elements possess both existential reality and a representational character. When, for example, the maiden, in 2:4 f., announces that she is faint with love and asks to be sustained with raisins and apples, she is calling for concrete food, to be sure, but *at the same time,* by her choice of fruits that are symbolic of love, she is indicating that only the satisfaction of her desires will bring her healing. To cite another instance, when the beloved speaks of awakening her lover who is asleep under the apple-tree (8:5), the tree is real enough, but, at the same time, it symbolizes her wish to rouse the dormant desire of her lover. When the girl declares, "I am a wall and my breasts are towers" (8:10), the simile is especially apt, because it expresses both her inaccessibility to the many suitors who are besieging her, and her maturity and readiness for love when her true lover appears.

Nor is the potency of symbolism exhausted by this trait alone. It is characteristic of the delicacy of the songs that the woman in each case expresses her desire for love by indirection. While a blunt avowal would repel by its crassness, the use of symbolism, which conceals as it reveals, heightens by its subtlety the charm of the sentiments expressed. Psycho-analytic theory has offered a highly plausible explanation for this powerful appeal of symbolism to the human spirit. According to psycho-analysis, the "unconscious" persistently seeks some avenue of expression which will elude the "censor" who stands guard over the conscious mind. Symbolism performs this liberating function for the unconscious admirably, because, in its very nature,

---

[135] Thus, in Palestinian Arabic, a girl deprived of her virginity is described as *maftûḥa* (see Stephan, p. 16). Cf. also the Talmudic phrase פתח פתוח מצאתי (Ket. 9b) as a charge of unchastity.

it expresses far more than it says; its nuances are at least as significant as its explications. Its overt meaning has nothing in it to arouse the vigilance of the censor, and meanwhile its deeper content is able to cross the threshold of consciousness.

Modern psychological research has also shed considerable light on the intimate relationship between love and pain. This connection is expressed in the great "Dream-Song" (5:2 to 6:3). When the love-sick maiden wanders through the city, in search of her lover, the watchmen beat her (5:7).

Stephan cites an old ḥaddâwiyye from Jaffa, which affords a striking parallel:[136]

> "The quarrel rose between me and him:
> They dragged me to the *sarai*;
> They beat me a thousand strokes;
> They beat me on my ankles."

An Egyptian love song of the New Kingdom[137] expresses the same theme of the lover's devotion in the face of physical attack:

> "I will not let go of thy love
> Even if I am beaten,
> As far as the land of Palestine with *shebet* and clubs
> And on to the land of Ethiopia with palm-ribs
> As far as the hills with sticks
> And unto the fields with cudgels."

The variations in date and geographical provenance do not exhaust the variety to be found within this small book. The songs reflect the simplicity of rustic scenes, the sophistication of the great city, the poverty of the shepherd's hut, and the luxury of the royal palace. Hence it is possible for one scholar to find in the book "the simplest kind of ballads scarcely touched by the polishing efforts of the self-conscious poet,"[138] while another declares that the Song is to be classed "as belles-lettres rather than as folk-songs," and finds them "only less artificial than the idylls of Theocritus."[139] Actually, the book contains both the simple and unrestrained outpourings of un-tutored love and the elaborated literary expressions of the same basic impulse.

[136] *Op. cit.*, p. 18.
[137] Cf. A. Erman, *op. cit.*, p. 241.
[138] Cf. Jastrow, *op. cit.*, p. 13.
[139] Cf. Pfeiffer, *op. cit.*, p. 711.

Frequently the point is made that the boldness of expression in the book with regard to sexual intimacy and bodily description is not in keeping with modern taste. It is true that the description of the maiden's charms in 7:3 is more explicit and franker than has been customary in Occidental poetry, but this passage is unique in the Song. Elsewhere, the description of physical beauty is frank without crassness. To evaluate it fairly, the Song should be judged against its Oriental background. Actually, its delicacy is at least as striking as its lack of inhibitions. The symbolism used in describing the manifestations of love throughout the book adds piquancy without offending. It should also be noted that some of the most outspoken passages are to be found in songs relating to married love.[140] Yet even here we have none of the crassly physical references to be found in the Akkadian love-charms,[141] in Sumerian love-poems,[142] or in contemporary Arabic love-songs.[143]

Esthetic standards are notoriously prone to change. In describing the beauty of a woman today, we would not think of her as resembling a city or a mare (1:9), yet we do compare a city to a woman,[144] and we refer to a beautiful horse by the feminine pronoun. A horse was, of course, not a beast of burden, but the cherished comrade of kings and nobles.[144a] Sociological and economic factors undoubtedly influence tastes in feminine pulchritude. The ancients liked their women large, as the Venus de Milo demonstrates and as is clear from the Song, even after allowance is made for poetic hyperbole (see 4:4; 7:5). Undoubtedly this taste for an ample woman reflected the emphasis upon child-bearing as woman's chief task. On the other hand, the modern preference for thin, "stream-lined" figures testifies to the present position of women as associates, and even as competitors,

---

[140] Thus 1:12, 13 and 7:3 f. both occur in poems where the lover is "king," i. e. the bridegroom (1:12; 7:6).

[141] Cf. Ebeling, "Liebeszauber," *passim*. See especially the direct references to the *membra* (pp. 11, 33) and to sexual congress (pp. 21, 43).

[142] See the Sumerian "Love Song to a King" (S. N. Kramer, in Pritchard, *op. cit.*, p. 496).

[143] Cf. Stephan, *op. cit.*, pp. 21, 39, for examples of such crudity in modern Arabic poetry.

[144] A striking instance where a city is compared to love occurs in Egyptian poetry:

"I will go to Memphis and say, 'Give me my sister tonight,
Memphis is a dish of love-apples, set before the Fair of Face.' "

(The last epithet is a name of Ptah, god of Memphis). Cf. Erman, *op. cit.*, p. 245.

[144a] See the description of the horse in Job 39:19 ff. and Horace, *Odes*, III, 2.

with men in all fields of activity in a society of small families, where child-bearing plays a considerably less important role. Yet in this area the French proverb has particular cogency: "Plus ça change, plus c'est la même chose." The love of a man for a maid is a perennially fresh theme in literature, because it is a constant of human nature.

XIV. SOME STYLISTIC TRAITS IN THE SONG

Our understanding of the Song of Songs is helped considerably when certain characteristics of style are kept in mind. One of these is the *use of quotations*, without any external formula or phrase to indicate that the words are being quoted. Elsewhere we have shown how widespread this usage is in Biblical, Rabbinical and Oriental literature generally.[145] Several passages in the Song are best explained as instances of this use of quotations.

In 1:7–8, Tur Sinai[146] plausibly explains v. 8 as the words of the shepherds who want to draw her affections away from her lover:

> Tell me, O thou whom I love,
> Where dost thou feed and rest thy flock at noon?
> Why should I be a wanderer
> Among the flocks of thy friends,
> *Who would mock me and say, if I asked about thee:*
> "If thou dost not know, O fairest among women,
> Go forth in the tracks of the flocks
> And feed thy kids near the shepherds' tents."

The closing verses of the Song, 8:13 f., are explained by Haller as containing the words that the lover wishes to hear from his beloved:

> O thou who sittest in the garden
> With friends listening,
> Let me hear thy voice
> *Saying to me,*
> "Hasten, my beloved, and be as a gazelle,
> Or as a young hart
> Upon the mountains of spices."

In 1:4, the third stich, "We will rejoice and be merry with thee," may well be the quotation of the words of the bridegroom to his

---

[145] Cf. "Quotations As a Literary Usage in Biblical and Oriental Literature," in *HUCA*, vol. 22 (1949); see also *KMW*, pp. 95 ff.

[146] *Op. cit.*, pp. 365 f.

beloved, who responds in the following stichs, "We shall inhale thy love more than wine."

This use of quotations without a *verbum dicendi* is illustrated in a popular modern Palestinian Arab song, current in several versions:[147]

"If you should visit me one night, O perfection of my
     happiness,
I would rejoice and mortify the envious (saying:),
"My friend regales me."

The use of similes and metaphors in the Song also requires a word of explanation. When the poet uses a figure of speech, he often continues to elaborate upon it for its own sake, without reference to the subject for the sake of which it was invoked. The figure, so to speak, develops its own momentum and has its own independent existence. Thus, in 4:2,

"Thy teeth are like a flock ready for shearing
Who have come up from washing,"

the second stich describes the sheep, without being related back to the teeth. Similarly, in 4:4,

"Like the tower of David is thy neck,
Built as a landmark,"

the second stich likewise refers not to the neck, but to the tower of David.

The difficulties and obscurities of the Song are due, in large measure, to the fact that it is an expression of a segment of Israelite life, which is largely unknown to us otherwise. Reference has already been made to variations in esthetic standards. These factors should caution us against facile emendations and transpositions in the text. Only in a small number of passages does emendation of the Masoretic text seem justified on the basis of our present state of knowledge.[148]

---

[147] Stephan, *op. cit.*, p. 60:

  *lô zurtani fard lêle yâ kamâl sa'di
  afraḥ v'akîd il-'azul: — "ḥubbi mhannîni."*

[148] The following changes from the Masoretic text underlie our version:
1:2 For יַשְׁקֵנִי read יָשְׁקֵנִי
3:6 For כְּתִימְרוֹת read בְּתִימְרוֹת (doubtful)
4:15 For גַּנִּים read גַּנִּי
5:13 For מִגְדְּלוֹת read מְגַדְּלוֹת
     For עֲרוּגַת read עֲרוּגוֹת
6:12 For שָׂמַתְנִי מַרְכְּבוֹת read שָׁם תְּנִי מֹרֶךְ בַּת
7:14 For דּוֹדִי read דּוֹדִי
8:2 For תְּלַמְּדֵנִי read וְאֶל חֶדֶר הוֹרָתִי (see the Commentary)

XV. The Song of Songs in Holy Writ

Undoubtedly, the allegorical interpretation of the Song of Songs, aided by the ascription of the book to King Solomon who is mentioned in the text, led to its inclusion in the Biblical canon. That Pharisaic Judaism admitted the book into the canon because it was "an ancient book, a religious book, and one that had always been religious"[149] as part of a pagan fertility cult, is unlikely to the point of impossibility. Had there been any recollection of such a use of the material, those who objected to the canonicity of the book would not have hesitated to mention it, and its chances for inclusion would have been nil.

The view against which Rabbinic Judaism levelled its strictures and which led to lengthy discussions as to its canonicity was the widely held literal interpretation, with which the Rabbis were very familiar, as has been noted. That all objections were overridden and the Song admitted into the canon indicates that on the subconscious level, at least, another factor operated, as was the case with Ecclesiastes:[150] a genuine affection for the book. It was this attitude which refused to permit its exclusion from Scripture, an act that would have spelled its ultimate destruction. As Jastrow well says: "It entered the canon not by vote, but because of its inevitable human appeal. Love is sacred even in passionate manifestations, when not perverted by a sophisticated self-analysis."[151]

The physical basis of love is extolled in the Song without shame or pruriency. Yet it serves as the foundation for the spiritual relationship, which is adumbrated in many an incidental phrase and reaches its climax in the great paean to love[152] in 8:7:

> Many waters can not quench love,
> Neither can the floods drown it.
> If a man would give all the substance of his house for love,
> He would be laughed to scorn.

---

[149] Cf. Meek, in Schoff, *op. cit.*, pp. 52 f.

[150] Cf. Gordis, *KMW*, pp. 121 f.

[151] *Op. cit.*, p. 16.

[152] Tur-Sinai, *op. cit.*, pp. 383 f., refers the "love" which is the subject in 8:7 not to the relationship of a maiden and her lover, but to the effort of an interloper to steal the affections of a married woman from her husband. The passage is interpreted to mean that it is impossible to make monetary restitution for this heinous sin. This is highly ingenious, but we find it unconvincing. There is a clear-cut reference to the wronged husband in Prov. 6:27 ff., which Tur-Sinai adduces as a parallel, but it is entirely lacking here.

It is in this sense that the modern reader, who is not likely to read it as an allegory, will echo Akiba's passionate description of the book as "the Holy of Holies," for it is, in Herder's words, "holy as a song of pure natural love, the holiness of human life."

Over and beyond its eternal youthfulness and inherent charm, the Song of Songs, precisely because it is within the canon of Scripture, serves to broaden the horizons of religion. It gives expression, in poetic and hence in deathless terms, to the authentic world-view of Judaism, which denies any dichotomy between body and soul, between matter and spirit, because it recognizes them both as the twin aspects of the great and unending miracle called life.

THE SONG OF SONGS, WHICH IS SOLOMON'S

I

THE CALL TO LOVE

In passionate accents, the beloved voices her desire for the presence of her bridegroom, who is here called "king," in accordance with a common West-Semitic and Jewish usage.

This song emanates not from the countryside, but from the city. Hence the background of many-chambered houses, the abundance of wine and oil and the presence of many maidens (1:2–4).

Let me drink of the kisses of his mouth,
For thy love is better than wine!
Thine oils are a delight to inhale,
Thy presence — as oil wafted about,
Therefore do the maidens love thee.

Draw me after thee, let us hasten —
The king has brought me to his chambers,
Saying, "We will rejoice and be merry with thee!"
We shall inhale thy love rather than wine!
As fine wine do they love thee.

II

THE RUSTIC MAIDEN

A country girl addresses the sophisticated women of the capital with a mixture of naivete and coquetry, of modesty and pride. Her skin, unlike that of the well-kept women of the capital, is dark. She has been exposed to the sun's rays, because she has been compelled to guard the vineyards of her brothers, who were angry with her. Their displeasure stemmed from the fact that she had left her own "vineyard" unguarded, being too prodigal with her favors (1:5–6).

Swarthy am I, but comely, O daughters of Jerusalem,
Swarthy as Kedar's tents,
Comely as Solomonic hangings.
Do not look askance upon me, for being swarthy,
For the sun has tanned me;
My brothers were incensed against me,
They set me a keeper over the vineyards;
But my own vineyard I did not keep.

III

TELL ME WHERE MY LOVE

The maiden pleads with her lover, to tell her where he is guarding his flocks. She gives him a gentle warning that if she must seek him herself, his fellow-shepherds are likely to make overtures for her affection (1:7–8).

Tell me, O thou whom I love,
Where dost thou pasture thy sheep,
Where dost thou let them lie at noon?
Why, indeed, should I be a wanderer
Among the flocks of thy comrades,
Who would say to me:
"If thou knowest not, fairest among women,
Follow the footprints of the sheep,
And pasture thy kids
Near the tents of the shepherds."

IV

BEDECKED IN CHARM

In this duet, the locale of which is southern Palestine, the "king" praises the beauty of his bride, bedecked in gold and silver ornaments, and compares her to a steed in Pharaoh's chariots. The comparison, somewhat strange to our habits of thought, is characteristically Semitic. It should be recalled that the horse was not a beast of burden in the Orient, but the cherished companion of kings and nobles in war and the chase. The bride responds by extolling the joys of love with her "king" (1:9–14).

THE BRIDEGROOM: To a steed in Pharaoh's chariots
Do I compare thee, my beloved.
Thy cheeks are beautiful with banglets,
Thy neck, with strings of jewels.
Golden beads shall we make thee
With studs of silver.

THE BRIDE: While the king was on his couch,
My nard gave forth its fragrance.
A bag of myrrh is my beloved,
Lying between my breasts.
A cluster of henna is my beloved to me
From the vineyards of En-gedi.

V

OUR WALLS ARE CEDARS

This simple lyric is of North-Israelite origin. The lovers make their tryst in the forest, with the cedars and cypresses as their home (1:15–17).

THE LOVER: Thou art fair, my beloved, thou art fair,
Thine eyes are doves.

THE BELOVED: Thou art handsome, my beloved, yea sweet,
And our couch is green.

BOTH: The beams of our house are cedars,
And our rafters are cypresses.

54-1758

VI

WHO IS LIKE MY LOVE

In this brief duet, the maiden describes her charms in modest terms, which the lover turns into a triumphant praise of her beauty. She counters by extolling his handsome presence, describing the joy she finds in his company (2:1–3).

THE MAIDEN: I am but a rose in Sharon,
      A lily of the valleys.

THE YOUTH: As a lily among thorns,
      So is my beloved among the young women.

THE MAIDEN: As an apple-tree among the trees of the
      wood,
      So is my love among the young men.
      Under its shadow I delight to sit,
      And its fruit is sweet to my taste.

VII

LOVE'S PROUD PROCLAMATION

The maiden proudly announces her love before all who are assembled in the tavern, and asks for refreshment, for she is faint through passion. She adjures the daughters of Jerusalem by a solemn oath to leave the lovers undisturbed, till their desire be spent (2:4-7).

He has brought me to the banquet-hall,
With his banner above me of love.
Strengthen me with dainties, sustain me with apples;
For I am love-sick.
His left hand is beneath my head,
While his right embraces me.
I adjure you, O daughters of Jerusalem,
By the gazelles and the hinds of the field,
That you disturb not, nor interrupt our love,
Until it be satiated.

VIII

THE TIME OF SINGING IS COME

This lyric is perhaps the most beautiful expression of love in the spring to be found in literature. It is worth noting that the point of origin is the city rather than the country. That nature discloses her charms primarily to the urban dweller rather than to the rustic has long been suspected. The appreciation of nature and the creation of nature-poetry are the products of urban culture, whether it be ancient Israel, the Hellenistic Age, the Silver Age of Roman literature, or the modern Romantic movement.

The city maiden, ensconced in her house, sees her lover coming to her and calling her to go out with him to the country-side, so that they may greet the spring in all its loveliness (2:8–13).

Hark! my beloved! here he comes,
Leaping over the mountains, skipping over the hills.
My beloved is like a gazelle or a young hart;
Behold, he stands behind our wall,
Looking through the windows,
Peering through the lattices.
My beloved spoke, saying unto me:
"Rise up, my love, my fair one, and come away.
For lo, the winter is past,
The rain is over and gone;
The flowers have appeared on the earth;
The time of singing is come,
And the voice of the turtle-dove is heard in our land.
The fig-tree puts forth her green fruits,
And the vines in blossom give forth their fragrance.
Arise, my love, my fair one, and come away."

IX

THE LOVER'S WELCOME

That a new song begins here seems clear. The beloved is here pictured as hiding among the cliffs, instead of being in her city home, and the lover calls upon her not to go out with him to the countryside, but to show herself to him. Her response is expressed cryptically. Little foxes have been devouring the vineyards already in bloom. Does she mean that young men have already found their way to her? (2:14–15).

THE LOVER: O my dove, in the clefts of the rock, in
　　　　　　the shadow of the cliff,
　　　　　　Let me see thy face, let me hear thy voice;
　　　　　　For sweet is thy voice, and thy face is
　　　　　　comely.

THE BELOVED: The foxes have seized us, the little foxes
　　　　　　that spoil the vineyards;
　　　　　　For our vineyard is in blossom.

X

SURRENDER

The maiden speaks of the love binding her and her lover, and invites him to taste the joys of love until dawn (2:16–17).

My beloved is mine, and I am his, who feeds among
    the lilies.
Until the day break, and the shadows flee,
Turn, my love, and be like a gazelle or a young hart
Upon the mountain of spices.

XI

THE DREAM OF THE LOST LOVER

The pathos of love's separation is movingly described in this song. Dreaming of her absent lover, the beloved wanders through the streets seeking him, until she finds him and holds him fast. She too, like the happy maiden in 2:7, adjures the daughters of Jerusalem not to disturb their love — but her reunion with her lover is only in a dream. The repetition of those passion-charged words highlights the pathos of the lovers' separation.

The sorrowful echo of an imaginary fulfillment recalls the scene in Christopher Marlowe's play, "Dr. Faustus," when the hero, in the last few hours before the Devil comes to claim his soul, repeats the words of Ovid, spoken by a lover in the midst of his revelry, "O lente, lente, currite noctis equi," "O slowly, slowly, run on, ye coursers of the night" (3:1-5).

On my couch at night I sought him whom I love,
Sought him, but found him not.
"I will rise now, and go about the city,
On the streets and highways,
I will seek him whom I love."
I sought him, but I found him not.
The watchmen making their rounds in the city found me.
"Have you seen him, whom I love?"
Scarcely had I passed them,
When I found him whom I love.
I held him, and would not let him go,
Until I had brought him into my mother's house,
Into the chamber of her that conceived me.
"I adjure you, O daughters of Jerusalem,
By the gazelles, and by the hinds of the field,
That you disturb not, nor interrupt our love,
Until it be satiated."

XII

A WEDDING SONG FOR SOLOMON

This song is the oldest datable unit in the collection. It was written to mark the ceremonies connected with King Solomon's marriage to a foreign princess, perhaps from Egypt, across the desert. Another example of a royal wedding hymn, not connected with Solomon, is to be found in Psalm 45. Here the arrival of the princess' elaborate entourage is described by the court poets (3:6–11).

Who is this coming from the wilderness,
Like thick clouds of smoke?
Perfumed with myrrh and frankincense,
With all powders of the merchant?
Behold, it is the litter of Solomon;
Sixty heroes round about it,
Of the heroes of Israel,
All skilled with the sword,
Expert in war.
Every man has his sword at his side
To ward off the terrors of the night.
A palanquin has the king made for himself,
Solomon, of Lebanon-wood.
He has made its pillars of silver,
Its inlay of gold,
Its seat of purple,
Its innermost parts being inlaid with ivory —
From the daughters of Jerusalem.
Go forth, O daughters of Zion,
And gaze upon king Solomon,
Arrayed in the crown with which his mother
        has crowned him
On his wedding-day,
On the day of his heart's gladness.

XIII

MY BELOVED IS PERFECT

A characteristic waṣf *in praise of the physical perfection of the beloved. Both the standard of feminine beauty that is extolled and the mode of expression that is employed are characteristic of the ancient Orient. See the Introduction for details* (4:1–7).

Thou art fair, my love, thou art fair!
Thine eyes are as doves behind thy veil,
Thy hair is as a flock of goats,
Streaming down from mount Gilead.
Thy teeth are like a flock ready for shearing,
Who have come from the washing,
All paired alike, and none missing among them.
Thy lips are like a scarlet thread
And thy mouth is comely;
Thy temples are like a slice of pomegranate,
Seen behind thy veil.
Thy neck is like the tower of David
Which is built as a landmark,
A thousand shields hanging upon it,
All the armour of the heroes.
Thy two breasts are like two fawns,
Twins of a gazelle,
Feeding among the lilies.
Until the day break
And the shadows flee,
I will get me to the mountain of myrrh,
And to the hill of frankincense.
Thou art all fair, my love;
And there is no blemish upon thee.

XIV

CALL FROM THE MOUNTAINS

From the Lebanon mountain range at the northern extremity of Israel comes the lover's call to his bride (4:8).

With me from Lebanon, my bride,
With me from Lebanon shalt thou come.
Leap from the top of Amana,
From the top of Senir and Hermon,
From the dens of the lions,
From the mountains of the leopards.

XV

LOVE'S ENCHANTMENT

The charm of the beloved has quite ravished her lover, who finds her presence more fragrant than wine and perfume, or the strong, clean smell of Lebanon's cedars, and her kisses sweeter than milk and honey. On the use of "sister" as a term of endearment in this song and succeeding ones, see the Introduction (4:9–11).

Thou hast ravished my heart, my sister, my bride;
Thou hast ravished my heart with one of thine eyes,
With one bead of thy necklace.
How fair is thy love, my sister, my bride!
How much better thy love than wine!
And the smell of thine ointments than all perfumes!
Thy lips, O my bride, drop honey —
Honey and milk are under thy tongue;
And the smell of thy garments is like the smell
    of Lebanon.

XVI

LOVE'S BARRIERS

In this dialogue, the lover praises the delectable qualities of his beloved, but complains that he finds her a closed garden, a sealed fountain. She responds by declaring that, on the contrary, she is a free-flowing fountain, and implies that her lover has been backward. She therefore calls upon the winds to waft her fragrance to him, that he may come and enjoy the fruit of his garden. He accepts her invitation with alacrity, and finally announces the joy of love's consummation (4:12 to 5:1).

THE LOVER: A closed garden is my sister, my bride;
A closed spring, a fountain sealed.
Thy branches are a garden of
    pomegranates,
With precious fruits,
Henna with nard,
Spikenard and saffron, cassia and
    cinnamon,
With all trees of frankincense;
Myrrh and aloes, with all the chief spices.

THE BELOVED: The fountain in my garden is a well of
    living waters,
Flowing down from Lebanon.
Awake, O north wind;
And come, O south;
Blow upon my garden,
Let its spices flow out,
Let my lover come into his garden,
And eat its delightful fruits.

THE LOVER: I have come into my garden, my sister,
  my bride;
I have gathered my myrrh with my spice;
Eaten my honeycomb with my honey;
Drunken my wine with my milk.

THE BELOVED: Eat, O my friend,
  Drink, yea, drink abundantly of love.

XVII

LOVE'S TRIAL AND TRIUMPH

The longest and most elaborate song in the collection takes the form of a dream-song. Within its framework, other patterns, like the search for the absent lover and the wasf *praising his person, are skillfully interwoven.*

The song reflects the sophistication and coquetry of the city maiden, whose artifices fall away before the power of love. The maiden is asleep, and in the dream she hears her lover knocking, begging to be admitted. She playfully answers that she has already retired for the night. Instead of continuing the badinage, as she expected, he leaves her doorway. Yearning for the sound of his voice, she runs out into the city streets, seeking for him everywhere. The city watchmen, mistaking her for a streetwalker, beat and wound her. She turns to the daughters of Jerusalem — everything is possible in a dream — and begs them to tell her lover that she is lovesick for him. How can they distinguish her lover from all others? Triumphantly she answers that he is unique for beauty, strength and charm. Impressed with her description, the daughters of Jerusalem offer to help find him. The maiden, however, feels that discretion is much the better part, and that too much help from them may be dangerous to her cause. She disclaims their assistance and joyously announces that her lover has already found his way to his garden. He is hers alone, and she is his (5:2 to 6:3).

I was asleep, but my heart was awake.
Hark! my love is knocking:
"Open to me, my sister, my love, my dove, my
  perfect one,
For my head is filled with dew,
My locks, with the drops of the night."
"I have already put off my coat,
Why should I put it on again;

I have washed my feet,
Why should I soil them?"
My beloved withdrew his hand from the door's opening,
And my heart was stirred for him.
I rose to open to my beloved,
And my hands were dripping with myrrh,
My fingers, with flowing myrrh,
Upon the handles of the bar.
I opened to my beloved,
But my beloved was gone and away.
My soul longed for his word;
I sought him, but could not find him;
I called him, but he gave me no answer.
The watchmen going about the city found me,
They struck me, they wounded me,
The keepers of the walls stripped my mantle from me.
"I adjure you, O daughters of Jerusalem,
If ye find my beloved,
What shall you tell him?
That I am faint with love."
"What is thy lover more than any other,
O fairest among women?
What is thy lover more than any other,
That thou dost so adjure us?"
"My beloved is fair and ruddy,
Pre-eminent above ten thousand.
His head is the finest gold,
His locks are curled, black as a raven.
His eyes are like doves, beside the water-brooks,
Bathing in milk, sitting at a brimming pool.
His cheeks are as beds of spices,
Exuding perfumes,
His lips are as lilies,
That drop with flowing myrrh.
His arms are rods of gold
Set with beryl,

His body is a column of ivory,
Overlaid with sapphires.
His legs are pillars of marble,
Set upon sockets of fine gold,
His appearance is like Lebanon,
Lordly as the cedars.
His mouth is sweetness itself,
He is altogether a delight.
This is my beloved, and this is my friend,
O daughters of Jerusalem."
"Where is thy lover gone,
O fairest among women?
Where has thy lover turned,
That we may seek him with thee?"
"My beloved is gone down to his garden,
To the beds of spices,
To feed in the gardens,
And to gather lilies.
I am my lover's,
And my beloved is mine,
As he feeds among the lilies."

XVIII

THE POWER OF BEAUTY

This is a very old waṣf, *which can be dated during the first half-century of the Divided Kingdom (between 930 and 880 B. C. E.). See the Introduction for details. The lover praises his beloved's beauty, by comparing her to the two capitals of the country, Jerusalem in the south and Tirzah in the north. The repetition of several phrases that are familiar to us from earlier songs in the collection is natural in popular poetry* (6:4–7).

Thou art beautiful, O my love, as Tirzah,
Comely as Jerusalem,
Awe-inspiring as these great sights!
Turn thine eyes away from me,
For they have overcome me.
Thy hair is as a flock of goats,
Streaming down from Gilead.
Thy teeth are like a flock of ewes,
Who have come up from the washing;
All paired alike and none missing among them.
Thy temple is a slice of pomegranate
Seen behind thy veil.

XIX

THE ONE AND ONLY

The lover has heard of the resplendent ladies in the royal court, but for him there is only one, unique and perfect, the favorite even of her mother among all her children. No wonder all women unite in praising her (6:8–9).

There are threescore queens,
And fourscore concubines,
And maidens without number.
But my dove, my pure one, is one alone,
The only one for her mother,
The choice of her that bore her.
Maidens saw her, and called her happy,
Even queens and concubines, and they praised her.

XX

LOVE'S DAWNING

For the lover, the beauty of the maiden can only be compared to the hosts of heaven. Spring is here, and he resolves to go down to his garden, to see the fruit-trees in blossom. There his beloved will let him enjoy her fragrance.

The last verse is incomprehensible in the accepted text. For the emendation on which our rendering is based, see the Commentary (6:10–12).

Who is she gazing forth like the morning star,
Fair as the moon,
Bright as the sun,
Awe-inspiring like these great sights?
I have come into the garden of nuts,
To look at the tender shoots of the valley,
To see whether the vine has budded,
And the pomegranates are in flower.
I am beside myself with joy,
For there thou wilt give me thy myrrh,
O noble kinsman's daughter!

XXI

THE MAIDEN'S DANCE

Among the Syrian peasants in our time, it is customary for the bride to perform a sword-dance on her wedding day. Our song has often been regarded as a Hebrew counterpart of this Syrian practice. This may well be the case, since the "king," or bridegroom, is mentioned in the song, though there is no reference to a sword in our text. What is certain is that the maiden is dancing, revealing both her grace of movement and her physical charms. She is referred to as the maid of Shulem, after a town (Biblical Shunem, modern Arabic, Sulem) which was famous for its beautiful women. This epithet "Shulammite" in Hebrew was mistaken for the proper name of a rustic maiden with whom Solomon fell in love.

The song begins with the company's call to her to turn, so that her comeliness may be observed. She modestly wonders what they can see in her. They proceed, however, to describe the beauty of her body in motion, from her dancing feet to the crowning glory of her tresses (7:1–6).

THE COMPANY: "Turn, turn, O maid of Shulem,
Turn, turn, so that we can see thee!"

THE MAIDEN: "What will you see in the maid of
Shulem?"

THE COMPANY: "Indeed, the counter-dance!
How beautiful are thy steps in sandals,
O nobleman's daughter!
The roundings of thy thighs are like
jewelled links,
The handiwork of a craftsman.
Thy navel is like a round goblet
In which the wine-mixture is not lacking.

Thy belly is like a heap of wheat,
Set about with lilies.
Thy two breasts are like two fawns,
Twins of a gazelle.
Thy neck is as a tower of ivory.
Thine eyes are pools in Heshbon,
At the gate of Bath-rabbim,
Thy nose is like the tower of Lebanon
Facing toward Damascus.
Thy head upon thee is like crimson,
And the hair of thy head like purple —
A king is held captive in its tresses!"

XXII

HOW DELIGHTFUL IS LOVE

In this rhapsody to love, the lover compares his chosen one to a slender and stately palm-tree and announces his intention of climbing up its branches and enjoying its delights (7:7–10).

The succeeding verses (7:11–14) may possibly constitute the beloved's reply. Since, however, our passage is not a plea directly addressed to the beloved, but rather a song of praise, and the next verses are not couched as a reply, it seems likelier that we have two independent songs here.

How fair and how pleasant art thou, love,
    with its delights!
Thy form is like a palm-tree,
Thy breasts, like clusters of grapes.
I said: "I will climb up into my palm-tree,
And take hold of its branches.
Let thy breasts be as clusters of the vine,
And the fragrance of thy face like apples,
For thy kiss is like the finest wine
That gives power to lovers,
And stirs the lips of the sleepers with desire."

XXIII

THE BELOVED'S PROMISE

*With a joyous affirmation of the love binding her and her
lover, the maiden calls upon him to come out into the fields
and vineyards, blooming in the glory of the spring. There,
she promises, she will give him her love (7:11–14).*

> I am my beloved's,
> And for me is his desire.
> Come, my beloved, let us go forth into the field,
> Let us lodge among the villages,
> And rise early for the vineyards.
> Let us see whether the vine has budded,
> Whether the vine-blossom has opened,
> And the pomegranates have flowered —
> There will I give thee my love.
> The mandrakes are giving forth their fragrance,
> And at our door are all sweet fruits,
> Both new and old —
> There will I give thee my love,
> Which I have laid up for thee.

XXIV

WOULD THOU WERT MY BROTHER

The maiden has been exposed to the taunts of neighbors and friends, when she has given public expression to her love. If only her lover were her foster-brother, raised in the same home! None could reproach her, then, if she were to kiss him in the street, lead him to her mother's home and drink wine at his side. In her reverie, she pictures the bliss in her lover's company, and calls upon the daughters of Jerusalem not to disturb her imagined ecstasy (8:1–4).

Would thou wert indeed my brother,
Who had suckled at my mother's breasts!
If I found thee outside, I could kiss thee;
Yet no one would despise me.
I would bring thee to my mother's house
Who had taught me,
I would give thee spiced wine to drink,
The juice of pomegranates.
His left hand would be beneath my head,
And his right hand would embrace me.
And I would exclaim,
"I adjure you, O daughters of Jerusalem:
Why should you disturb or interrupt our love
Until it be satiated?"

XXV

LOVE UNDER THE APPLE-TREE

This passage, which may be fragmentary, is not very clear, principally because of the symbolism employed. It seems to be a duet, where the company greets the advent of the maiden leaning on her lover. She, however, has no ear for their words, but addresses her lover. She reminds him that she woke him from his sleep under the apple-tree. It was at the self-same spot that he had come into the world, because of the love of his father and mother. The apple-tree, a familiar erotic symbol, is, as Jastrow notes, the sexual passion which passes from one generation to the next. The maiden is apparently calling him to respond to her love (8:5).

THE COMPANY: Who is this coming up from the wilderness,
Clinging to her beloved?

THE BELOVED: Under the apple-tree I woke thee,
There thy mother gave thee birth,
Yea, there she who bore thee brought
thee forth.

XXVI

THE SEAL OF LOVE

The maiden can not bear any separation from her lover. She therefore pleads to be as close to him as his seal. The ancients carried their seals either as a ring on the finger or as a necklace near the heart.

The frank and unabashed avowal of love throughout the book reaches its impressive climax here where it is described as a mighty force, the very flame of God. Thus the basic truth underlying the Song of Songs is emphasized, that natural love is holy (8:6–7).

Set me as a seal upon thy heart,
As a seal upon thine arm,
For love is strong as death,
Passion is unyielding as the grave.
Its flashes are flashes of fire,
A flame of God.
Many waters can not extinguish love,
Nor can the floods sweep it away.
If a man gave all the wealth of his house
In exchange for love,
He would be laughed to scorn.

XXVII

THE RAMPARTS OF LOVE

The young maiden is surrounded by suitors who complain that she is not ready for love and marriage. Their determination to break down her resistance they express by using the formula of an oath (see the Introduction). If she remains obdurate, like the wall of a city, they will lay siege to her. This they plan to do in approved military fashion, by building around her another temporary embankment, from which they will launch the "attack." That their intentions are not hostile is clear from the materiel *of war that they intend to employ in their campaign, silver and cedar-wood. These expensive goods probably symbolize the gifts that they are showering upon her.*

She answers that she is indeed like a wall, impregnable to their importunities, but not because she is too young for love. On the contrary, she is ready for the great experience, but only with him whom she loves and strives to please above all others (8:8–10).

THE SUITORS: We have a little sister,
But she has no breasts.
What shall we do with our sister,
On this day when she is being spoken for?
If she be a wall,
We will build a turret of silver against her;
If she be a gate,
We will besiege her with boards of cedar.

THE MAIDEN: I am a wall,
And my breasts are like towers,
Therefore am I in my lover's eyes
As one finding favor.

XXVIII

THE FINEST VINEYARD

The genuine joys of love are graphically contrasted with the illusory satisfactions of wealth. The lover recalls that King Solomon owned a large and fruitful vineyard containing a thousand vines. It was worked by tenant-farmers, who received one-fifth of the income for their labor. The lover may be poor in money, yet he is far richer than Solomon, for he possesses a priceless treasure, the vineyard of his beloved (8:11–12).

Solomon owned a vineyard at Baal Hamon
Which he gave over to tenants.
For its fruit one would give
A thousand pieces of silver.
But my vineyard, my very own, is before me.
You, Solomon, are welcome to your thousand,
And your vine-tenders to their two hundred!

XXIX

LET ME HEAR THY VOICE

The beloved, sitting in the garden, is surrounded by her companions. Her lover pleads with her to invite him to enjoy the delights of love. As he quotes the words that he wishes to hear her say, he employs the familiar figures of the young deer and the fragrant mountain to symbolize the lover and his beloved (8:13–14).

> Thou dwelling amid the gardens,
> While thy companions are listening,
> Let me hear thy voice, saying to me,
> "Make haste, my beloved,
> And be like a gazelle or a young hart
> Upon the mountains of spices."

COMMENTARY

1:1. The verse is the title of the book, added by the editor. Hence the use of the classical relative *'ašer* instead of *še* employed throughout the book (e. g. 1:6; 5:8; 6:5, etc.). The post-Exilic editor accepts the Solomonic theory of authorship, which made the acceptance of the book into the canon possible. Hence שיר השירים meant for him "the best of songs," and is a superlative like קדש הקדשים, "holy of holies," הבל הבלים, "vanity of vanities" (Eccl. 1:2), מלך המלכים, "king of kings," as it was for Rabbi Akiba, "For all the writings are holy, but the Song of Songs is the Holy of Holies" (M. Yad. 5:3).

1:2. Read, with many moderns, יַשְׁקֵנִי. The change of person in the song is a characteristic of Biblical style; cf., *inter alia*, Micah 7:19. There is, therefore, no need to assume more than two characters in this song or to emend the vowels or suffixes in order to create a non-Biblical standard of consistency.

1:3. שָׁמֶן תּוּרַק is best taken as "oil wafted about," literally "emptied, poured forth" (cf. LXX, V), though שָׁמֶן is elsewhere masculine. Thus הָמוֹן, generally masculine, is feminine only in Job 31:34 and Eccl. 5:9 (reading תְּבוֹאֵהוּ for תְּבוֹאֶה). See *KMW, ad loc.* תְּהוֹם, generally feminine, is masculine in Ps. 42:8; 104:6 ("The deep — Thou hast covered it as with a garment") and in Job 28:14. Common in gender are מחנה, כיס, שמש, דרך, etc. There is, therefore, no need to read תַּמְרוּק (cf. Esth. 2:3, 9, 12) or מוּרָק (*BH*) or מוּזָק, "purified" (Rothstein). שְׁמֶךָ, "your name, being, presence." Cf. the figurative use of "the Name" for the presence or essence of God. On the assonance of *šem* and *šemen*, cf. Eccl. 7:1, and *KMW, ad loc.*

1:4. נַזְכִּירָה, not "we shall praise" but "we shall inhale"; on this meaning of the root, cf. Lev. 24:7; Isa. 66:3; Hos. 14:8; Ps. 20:4 (cf. I Sam. 26:19), as Ibn Janah recognized long ago. Hence there is no need to emend to נִשְׁכְּרָה, "we shall be drunk." אהבוך, 3rd person plural, is impersonal; cf. וגללו, Gen. 29:8; hence, "they love you, i. e. you are loved."

The traditional rendering for מישרים אהבוך, "rightly have they loved thee" (LXX, V, Rashi), is syntactically dubious and out of context. Deleting the phrase is a too easy solution; it destroys the rhythmic pattern which consists of 2 stichs (v. 2) followed by 3 (v. 3) and then of 3 stichs, followed by 2 (v. 4). What is required in the context is a reference to another element in the triad of wine, women and song. Accordingly, Ibn Ezra equates the word with "wine," in favor of which the parallelism may be adduced, as well as the occurrence of the word in connection with wine three times (here, in 7:10, and in Prov. 23:31). In the two other passages, the noun occurs with הלך: הלך לדודי למישרים and יתהלך במישרים; the noun, therefore, would seem to be the purpose or effect of the wine-drinking; see the Commentary on 7:10 for another suggestion. Here it may mean "strong wine" or refer to a special variety. Both because of the parallelism and the better syntax, it may be better to render the stich: "As fine wine do they love thee." On the other hand, Tur-Sinai (*op. cit.*, 369) interprets the word to mean "sexual potency," on the basis of Akkadian *mushartu*, which he interprets as "paramour," and *musharu*, "membrum virile." However, the etymology which he proposes is not borne out by the Akkadian (cf. M. Weir, *Lexicon of Accadian Prayers*, pp. 39, 221). Ben Jehudah also gives the word a sexual connotation, but his derivation is likewise doubtful (*Thesaurus*, VI, 2980 f.). Our word may, however, well mean "vigor, virility, strength," on the basis of indigenous Hebrew usage. Cf. the common Rabbinic phrase יְישֶׁר כֹּחַ, "May your strength be firm" (B. B. 14b), and the Biblical source *Sefer Hayašār*, probably "The Book of Heroes" (Josh. 10:13; II Sam. 1:18). The stich may therefore mean, "For thy manliness do they love thee."

1:5. The verse exhibits "alternate parallelism," a, b, a', b' (cf. Ex. 29:27; Deut. 22:25–27; Hos. 3:5; Ps. 33:20 f.; Ps. 113:5–6; Eccl. 5:17 ff., and cf. Gordis, "Al Mibneh Hashirah Haivrit Haqedumah," in *Sefer Hashanah Liyhude Amerika*, 1944, pp. 151 f., and *KMW*, p. 246). The opening stich does not mean "dunkel und doch hell" and is not a reference to the moon-goddess (against Hal., Wit.). Nor is the view that *šelōmōh* here refers to an Arab tribe *Shalmah* (e. g., T. H. Gaster, in *Commentary*, vol. 13, April, 1952, p. 322) acceptable. Not only does this hypothesis propose a strange meaning for a common Hebrew name, creating a *hapax legomenon*, but it destroys the alternate parallelism of the verse, "swarthy" being completed by "tents of Kedar," and "comely" by "Solomonic curtains." Since the first stich is antithetic and not synonymous, "swarthy but comely," the second must follow suit. Similarly, in Ps. 113:5–6, המנביהי לשבת המשפילי לראות בשמים ובארץ. The tents of the Bedouins, woven of goatskins, are dark-brown or black, and would be particularly familiar to the country-dwellers. "Solomon's curtains" is a generic term like זקן אהרן, Ps. 133:2, "an Aaronic beard;" cf. a "Van Dyke beard," "Louis Quatorze furniture," etc.

1:6. נְחֲרוּ, from חרה, a variant vocalization for נֶחֱרוּ; cf. the reverse phonetic process in Judg. 5:28, אֶחֲרוּ for אָחֲרוּ (against Hal.). For the vineyard as a symbol of the person of the beloved, cf. Isa. 5:1 f.;

Song 2:15; 8:12. The last-named passage, as here, employs "vineyard" in both the literal and the symbolic meanings.

1:7. שַׁלָּמָה, literally, "for why?", a Hebrew equivalent for the Aramaic דְּלְמָא, "lest," the use of *še* being principally, but not exclusively, North Israelite. Cf. אֲשֶׁר לָמָה (Dan. 1:10). כְּעֹטְיָה a) has been rendered "wayward woman," from the verb עטה I, "cover, wrap" (cf. I Sam. 28:14), hence "a robed woman, sign of a harlot" (cf. Gen. 38:14), and b) from עטה II, "delouse" (cf. Jer. 43:12 LXX; Von Gall, *ZATW*, 24, p. 105). It is best taken as a metathesis or a scribal error for טֹעִיָה (Sym., P, V, Tar.), "wandering one." The Kaph is asseverative, "Why indeed should I be a wanderer"; cf., for example, Num. 11:1, and see Gordis, in *JAOS*, vol. 63, 1943. The usage occurs again in our book in 8:1 and probably in 7:1.

1:8: The verse is a quotation of the speech of the shepherd's comrades used without a formula of citation, as Tur-Sinai recognizes, p. 366. On the entire usage of quotations, cf. R. Gordis, in *HUCA*, 1949.

1:9. On the Judean origin of this song and on this type of simile, see the Introduction. לְסֻסָתִי, "to a mare," ·with paragogic Yod; cf. Lam. 1:1.,

1:12. עַד, "while, so long as"; cf., for example, Job 1:18. בִּמְסִבּוֹ, not "table," but "couch"; cf. the Mishnaic use of הֵסֵב, "to recline."

1:14. בְּכַרְמֵי, perhaps "from the vineyards," rather than "in the vineyards"; cf. this meaning of Beth in Ugaritic. En-gedi, on the western shore of the Dead Sea, was famous for its vineyards; cf. Pliny, *Historia Naturalis*, XII, 14 and 24.

1:15. The deletion of עֵינַיִךְ יוֹנִים deprives the verse of its third stich. Note the three stichs in the next verse.

1:16. עַרְשֵׂנוּ, generally rendered "couch," may possibly mean "arbor." Cf. M. Kil. 6:1, עָרִיס. Deleting the third stich is unjustified. See v. 15.

1:17. קֹרוֹת בָּתֵּינוּ is the plural of קוֹרַת בֵּיתֵנוּ, formed on the Mishnaic model, where the plural of בֵּית כְּנֶסֶת is בָּתֵּי כְנֵסִיּוֹת (Ehr.). Hence the MT is to be rendered, not "the beams of our houses," but "the beams of our house." בְּרוֹתִים, a dialectic pronunciation for the classical בְּרוֹשִׁים, probably influenced by the Aramaic; cf. *sibōleth-šibbōleth*, Judg. 12:6, and see the Introduction and note 78. It is the cypress (I. Low) or the Phoenician juniper-tree (Koehler, *Lexicon*, s. v., according to Pliny, XII, 78).

2:1. חֲבַצֶּלֶת has been identified with the narcissus (Dalman), the *colchicum autumnale*, a flower of pale lilac-color (I. Löw), the saffron (Jastrow), and the rose (Tar., Ibn Janah, Ibn Ezra). שׁוֹשַׁנָּה, generally rendered "lily," is probably a red or dark purple flower; cf. 5:13. שָׁרוֹן, from יְשָׁרוֹן, "a valley, plain," was originally a common noun, and then was applied to the fertile central valley in Palestine, a process paralleled by *Carmel*; cf. the Commentary on 7:6.

2:2. בָּנוֹת = "girls"; cf. Prov. 31:29. On רַעְיָתִי, "beloved," see the Introduction, sec. XI.

2:3. חִמַּדְתִּי וְיָשַׁבְתִּי, "I delight to sit." Cf. Deut. 1:5; Hos. 5:11 for examples of this paratactic variant of the complementary infinitive.

2:4. וְדִגְלוֹ עָלַי אַהֲבָה, a difficult phrase which may perhaps contain a reference to a custom unfamiliar to us today. The traditional rendering, "His shield" (so Hal.) or, "his banner over me is love," is a bold and striking figure. The emendation וְדִגְלוּ, taken as an imperative plural verb, "serve me with love," on the basis of the Akkadian *dagâlu* (Del., Jastrow), does not commend itself, because we expect a singular verb addressed to the lover and, in addition, the preposition is unhebraic.

2:5. אֲשִׁישׁוֹת, "dainties," perhaps "raisin-cakes" (see Hos. 3:1). רַפְּדוּנִי, not "spread out" (Job 17:13; 41:22), but "strengthen," on the basis of the Arabic (Ibn Ezra, JPS). There is no need to change the imperative verbs to the perfect singular, "he has strengthened me" (against Hal.), since she is addressing the company in the banquet-hall. Note the plural in v. 7. Raisin-cakes, which were used in fertility rites (cf. Hos. 3:1), served, like the apple, as an erotic symbol on the subconscious level, while on the conscious level they refer literally to a source of physical refreshment. See the Introduction, sec. XIII.

2:7. On the oath and the symbolism employed, see the Introduction. תָּעִירוּ and תְּעוֹרְרוּ most naturally mean "arouse, stir up love" (JPS), on the basis of which Bettan interprets the passage to mean that the maiden opposes rousing love by artificial means in favor of gentle, natural love. This is not likely. Not only is there no reference to these artificial means in the text, but the context implies that she is already experiencing passionate love in all its fullness. Hence the verbs are best rendered "disturb, i. e. interfere with love" (so most commentators). עַד שֶׁתֶּחְפָּץ, "until love wishes" (*scilicet* to be disturbed, because it has been satisfied).

2:8. קוֹל = "hark." Cf. Gen. 4:10.

2:9. This verse is replete with Aramaisms and late Hebrew words. For כֹּתֶל, a *hapax legomenon* in the Bible, see the Targum to Lev. 1:15; for חֲרַכִּים see the Targum on Prov. 7:6. מַשְׁגִּיחַ is also an Aramaism; cf. Isa. 14:16; Ps. 33:14.

מֵצִיץ, in earlier Hebrew "sprout" (cf. Ps. 90:6) and "shine" (Ps. 132:18), here means "look, peep"; cf. the Mishnaic usage בן עזאי הציץ

ונפגע, "Ben Azzai looked in and was wounded" (M. Ḥag. 13:2). For a parallel semantic development, cf. the German *glänzen*, English *glance*.

2:10. The opening stich can not be deleted (against Hal.), as it leaves only one stich in the verse. Its presence militates strongly against the dramatic theory.

2:11. סְתָו, "winter," a *hapax legomenon*, is an Aramaism; cf. the Targum on Gen. 8:22, where it renders חֹרֶף. Some manuscripts and editions read סתו Kethib, סתיו Qere, an instance of the original function of the Kethib-Qere formula as a guide to the reader; see Gordis, *The Biblical Text in the Making* (Philadelphia, 1937).

2:12. On זְמִיר see the Introduction, note 30.

2:13. סְמָדַר, "in blossom," has Aramaic and Mandaic cognates, but no satisfactory etymology.

2:14. חֲגָוֵי, singular חֲגָה or חָגָה (cf. קָצֶה and קַצְוֵי), has the basic meaning "break, crack." It is used literally here, and figuratively in Isa. 19:17 in the meaning "destruction, calamity." מַדְרֵגוֹת, the terraces dug into the hillside for purposes of cultivation. Cf. Ezek. 38:20 for its use parallel to הָרִים.

2:15. The verse is patently symbolic. If the vineyard represents the maiden, the young foxes may be the young men who lay siege to her. אֶחֱזוּ is generally regarded as the imperative Qal, and the verse is then given two diametrically opposite interpretations: 1) "Catch the little foxes for us," a plea to save her chastity (so most commentators); and 2) "Take us, you little foxes," a plea for love (so Jast., Hal.). While the second view is far more appropriate to the theme, it is not satisfactory. In v. 14, the lover pleads to see his beloved; she is hardly likely to respond by calling upon many young men to take her. Even if verses 14 and 15 be treated as unrelated, the whole spirit of the *Song* militates against the idea of promiscuity in love, for everywhere the unique relationship of the pair involved is emphasized (cf. 6:9; 8:8 ff.; 8:11 ff.), while we do find complaints by the maiden of advances made by other youths, which she rejects (cf. 1:6 f.; 8:10). We prefer, there- fore, to regard אֶחֱזוּ as a perfect and to render the entire clause as "Little foxes have seized us." Nor is it necessary to revocalize the verb as אֶחֱזוּ, if it be recognized as a Piel, which occurs in Job 26:9, מְאַחֵז פְּנֵי כִסֵּה. On this form of the Piel perfect instead of the usual אִחֲזוּ, cf. Judg. 5:28, אֶחֱרוּ, the broader vocalization being due to the gutturals. לָנוּ is to be construed as the direct object; cf. Lev. 19:18; II Sam. 3:30. כְּרָמֵינוּ is a plene spelling for the singular: "our vineyard."

2:17. עַד שֶׁיָּפוּחַ הַיּוֹם, "until the day blows, i. e. in the morning"; note the parallelism, "and the shadows flee." On the night as the season for love, which really requires no Biblical references, cf. Prov. 7:18. It cannot mean "until evening," nor can the phrase "and the shadows flee" refer to nightfall, when the shadows lengthen and fade (against Bettan), since the context refers not to the lover's departure, but to his enjoyment of love. The gazelle and the hart are symbols of the lover. The precise meaning of הָרֵי בָתָר is not clear. It has been 1) emended to הָרֵי בְשָׂמִים, "hills of spices" (cf. 8:14); 2) interpreted to *mean* "spices"; 3) emended to read הָרֵי הַמּוֹר, "hills of myrrh" (Jastrow); and 4) taken as a geographical reference to Bether (or Betar) in Judah (AV, RV), later the scene of Bar Kochba's heroic but fruitless Third War against Rome (132–35 C. E.). Hal. suggests that the place-name may have been derived from an aromatic plant, so that the phrase may virtually mean "spices" in our passage.

3:1. While Jastrow deletes בִּקַּשְׁתִּיו וְלֹא מְצָאתִיו, Hal. adds קְרָאתִיו וְלֹא עָנָנִי, following the LXX. Actually, the LXX's reading here is an example of "leveling," to bring our passage into agreement with 5:6. Neither change is necessary, the two dream-songs being similar but not identical examples of this genre. The MT is therefore to be preferred.

3:3. Reading מָצָאתִי for the opening word is unnecessary; in fact the MT is superior (against Ehr., Hal.).

3:5. This refrain is often deleted on the ground that it is appropriate to a genuine meeting of the lovers, but not to a dream. See the Introductory Comment on this song for the psychological appropriateness of the oath both here and in 8:4.

3:6. כְּתִימְרוֹת עָשָׁן, "like pillars of smoke," a reference to the dust of the procession traveling across the desert. In Joel 3:3, the phrase alludes to the pillar of cloud which accompanied the Israelites in the wilderness (Ex. 13:21 f.). Perhaps we should read בְּתִימְרוֹת, "with pillars of smoke," which would refer either to the smoke-wreaths of the campfire at night, or possibly to the smoke of incense burned in the bride's honor. רוֹכֵל, "merchant"; cf. קופת הרוכלים (B. Giṭ. 67a). The root is a metaplastic form for רגל, "go on foot"; hence both roots develop the secondary connotation of "tale-bearing, slander"; cf. Jer. 9:3; Ps. 15:3.

3:7. On the "Aramaic" form שֶׁלִשְׁלֹמֹה and on the usage of pronominal anticipation, see Intr., sec. VIII and n. 80. The first two letters of שלשלמה may be a dittography.

3:8. אֲחֻזֵי חֶרֶב, the participle passive, is here used with middle force; cf. חָגוּר in Judg. 18:11, and such Mishnaic forms as סבור, מדומה, "thinking," etc. On the basis of the Akkadian, Perles interprets אחז as "taught, skilled"; cf. the parallelism. The "terrors of the night" may refer to evil spirits rampant particularly in those hours, or to desert bandits, who might be tempted to attack the richly laden caravan of a royal princess going to her wedding.

3:9. On the various foreign etymologies proposed for אַפִּרְיוֹן, see the Introduction and note 74. It is probably Sanskrit in origin. The Talmud uses the Biblical word occasionally (B. Sotah 49a), but more often the Aramaic פּוּרְיָא. In spite of the accents, the caesura belongs after הַמֶּלֶךְ; cf. Num. 23:7, where the pause comes after בָּלָק, likewise against the accents. On the parallelism, see the Introduction.

3:10. רְפִידָתוֹ, literally, "its bedding, inlay." מֶרְכָּבוֹ must be "the seat" rather than the "body" (Jast.). תּוֹכוֹ רָצוּף אַהֲבָה, generally rendered: "its parts are inlaid with love," is unsatisfactory (in spite of such instances of the adverbial accusative as Hos. 14:5, אֹהֲבֵם נְדָבָה, "I should love them freely"). The context requires a concrete substance, as the parallelism indicates, and most scholars accept Graetz's emendation הָבְנִים, "ivory," for אַהֲבָה (cf. Ezek. 27:15). Tur-Sinai proposes הַבִּים, from שֶׁנְהַבִּים (cf. I Kings 10:22). He bases his proposed vocable on the Aramaic יב for the place-name "Elephantine." "The daughters of Jerusalem" are the ladies of its court who prepared the decorations of the palanquin.

3:11. Crowns were worn even by ordinary grooms and brides, until the defeats sustained in the War against Rome in 70, when they were abandoned as a sign of mourning (cf. B. Sotah 49a). Hence the Rabbinic proverb חתן דומה למלך (*Pirke deRabbi Eliezer*, chap. 16). The Vav of וּבְיוֹם need not be deleted (against Ehr.). On its use in parallel stichs with no sense of addition, cf. Zech. 9:9, עָנִי וְרֹכֵב עַל־חֲמוֹר, וְעַל־עַיִר בֶּן־אֲתֹנוֹת. Here the failure to recognize the usage led to unusual consequences (cf. Matt. 21:2, 7). There is no need to transpose the order of the last four stichs (against Rothstein, Jast.).

4:1. There is no need to read עֵינַיִךְ כְּיוֹנִים (against Hal.). Much of the power of Biblical poetry derives from its directness, its preference for the metaphor over the simile, for the noun over the adjective.

גלשׁ, "trail down." The root is used in Rabbinic Hebrew of bubbling, boiling water (Pes. 37b) and of luxuriant tresses (Midrash Cant. Rab. 4:3).

4:2. The participle passive הַקְּצוּבוֹת has a gerundive force, "ready to be sheared," as Ehr. noted. Cf. Ps. 137:8, הַשְּׁדוּדָה, "destined to be despoiled." מַתְאִימוֹת, a Hiphil of condition, literally, "all in twins," a reference to the evenness of the two rows of teeth.

4:4. A large neck, like a prominent nose (cf. 7:5), was a mark of beauty to the ancients. Nonetheless, it is not the neck, but the tower of David, which is described as having room for a thousand shields. Shields were hung on towers for decoration and storing while not in active use; cf. Ezek. 27:11. On this use of similes in the *Song*, see the Introduction.

לְתַלְפִּיוֹת is an ancient crux, which the LXX did not understand and therefore transliterated (ϵἰς θαλπιώθ). The word has been rendered variously: 1) as "maneuvers," from the root אלף, "teach"; 2) as "landmark," from the same root (Ibn Janah); 3) as "armory" (AV, Jast.); 4) as "turrets," from תֵּל פִּיוֹת (?), "heap of points" (AV); 5) as "for looking afar off," from the Greek τηλῶπος (Graetz). It is noteworthy, however, that the LXX did not recognize it as such, and the Tav generally reproduces the Greek Theta, not the Tau; 6) by metathesis and revocalization it is read לִתְלוֹת יְפִי, "to hang beautiful things upon" (Tur-Sinai, who compares Ezek. 27:11, שִׁלְטֵיהֶם תָּלוּ; 7) Read לִפְתִילוֹת, which is taken to mean "built according to the (proper) lines," from פְּתִילָה, "thread" (Kuhn, Hal.). None of these views is strikingly persuasive.

4:5. שְׁנֵי is deleted by Jastrow, but this destroys the rhythm of the verse. The presence of the numeral emphasizes that both are alike.

4:6. There is no ground for eliminating this verse as a doublet of 2:17 (against Hal.). Refrains with variations are common in folk poetry. Nor need vv. 6 and 7 be reversed in order (against Rothstein, Jast.). The song ends with the theme with which it begins (v. 1), but with a slight variation in the refrain. This change in the refrain is a common characteristic of Biblical poetry; cf. Ps. 49:13, 21; Job 28:12, 20. The "mountain of myrrh" and the "hill of frankincense" are obvious symbols for the body of the beloved.

4:8. This verse may be a fragment of a song emanating from the mountain-ranges lying to the north of Israel. It is not necessary to emend the first אִתִּי to אֲתִי, "come" (against Hal.). The lover emphasizes "with me"; note the word-order. תָּשׁוּרִי is better derived not from שׁור, "look," but from the homonym "leap" (Aramaic שׁוּר; Arabic سار). It occurs in Hos. 13:7. On the parallelism of "come" and "leap," cf. 2:8. It is, therefore, unnecessary to read תָּסוּרִי with Hal.

אֲמָנָה here refers to the mountain from which the rivers Amana and Parpar flow (II Kings 5:12). While Deut. 3:9 and 4:48 identify Hermon, Sirion, Senir, and Sion, I Chron. 5:23 apparently distinguishes between Senir, Hermon (and Baal Hermon), as does our passage. The names may refer to different peaks. Leopards are still to be found in the Lebanon range, but lions are now extinct.

4:9. לִבַּבְתִּנִי, a privative Piel: "thou hast stolen my heart away"; cf. דִּשֵּׁן, שֵׁרֵשׁ, עִקֵּר. Ibn Janah interprets the verb as "pierced my heart," based on the Mishnaic עורות לבובין, "pierced skins" ('Ab. Zarah 2:3). The Kethib באחד is a scribal error for בְּאַחַת, which is the reading (not the correction) of the Qere; cf. Gordis, *The Biblical Text in the Making — A Study of the Kethib-Qere* (Philadelphia, 1936). The error was induced by the following phrase. In בְּאַחַד עֲנָק the word-order is an Aramaism, which penetrated Hebrew to some degree. Cf. Neh. 4:11, בְּאַחַת יָדוֹ. עֲנָק has two meanings: 1) "neck" (cf. Aramaic עוּנקא), hence "with one turn of thy neck" (Jast.); 2) "jewel" (cf. Prov. 1:9), hence "with one jewel." The latter is preferable here. מִצַּוְּרֹנַיִךְ is a defective spelling for מִצַּוְּארֹנָיִךְ. The noun צַוְּרוֹן is a derivative of צַוָּאר, "neck," with which the Versions and many commentators have confused it. It means not "neck," but "ornament for the neck, necklace." In modern Hebrew it is aptly used for "collar."

4:11. On the fragrance of the beloved's garments, cf. Ps. 45:9. The smell of Lebanon-wine is mentioned in Hos. 14:7; here the reference is to its cedars.

4:12. The two phrases גַּן נָעוּל and גַּל נָעוּל have often been regarded as identical. Thus the Versions read גַּן for the less familiar גַּל (LXX, P, V, also the Midrash). This is accepted by Kittel, *BH*, and by others who overlook the process of "leveling" here at work. Conversely, Hal. reads גַּל נָעוּל at the beginning of the verse and then deletes the second phrase as a dittography. Actually, the MT is in perfect order. The two figures of a sealed garden and a closed fountain are both highly appropriate for expressing the idea that the lover is being denied access to the delightful person of his beloved. Both themes are taken up later in the maiden's response (vv. 15–16). Note, too, that גַּל נָעוּל — a "sealed spring" (cf. Josh. 15:19; Judg. 1:15) — is an ideal transition-word between גַּן, which precedes it and which it resembles in sound, and מַעְיָן, which follows it and which it resembles in meaning. Moreover, the meter (2:2:2:2) effectively disposes of the effort to delete any part of the verse (against Jast.).

4:13. שְׁלָחַיִךְ, apparently "branches"; cf. Isa. 16:8. Hal. plausibly refers it to the arms or bosom. מֶגֶד, "blessing, sweetness"; cf. Deut. 33:13. The spices mentioned in these verses include several imports from the East. See the Introduction and note 75.

4:15. The Masoretic reading מַעְיָן גַּנִּים makes this verse a continuation of the lover's speech, but it then contradicts v. 12, for the beloved is here described as "a well of *flowing* water," while above she is called "a *sealed* fountain." It is therefore better to emend to מַעְיָן גַּנִּי, "the fountain of my garden" (so Budde, Ehr., Hal., *BH*), so that v. 13 contains the lover's complaint, v. 15, her denial of his charge, and v. 16 her invitation to him to enjoy his garden's delights.

5:1. אָרִיתִי, "I gather"; cf. Ps. 80:13. יַעַר = "honey-comb." The closing stich, אִכְלוּ רֵעִים שְׁתוּ וְשִׁכְרוּ דּוֹדִים, has occasioned much difficulty, since the lover is not likely to invite his friends to enjoy the delights of his beloved. Hence Ehr. emends it to the singular by five changes, אֱכֹל רֵעִי שְׁתֵה וּשְׁכַר דּוֹדִי, "Eat, my friend, drink abundantly, my beloved," while Hal. changes the text even more drastically to the feminine singular: אִכְלִי רַעְיָתִי שְׁתִי וְשִׁכְרִי דוֹדִים, "Eat, my beloved, drink abundantly of love." Others delete the stich entirely or regard it as a fragment of a drinking song now out of place (Jast.). On the occasional use of the plural for the singular in modern Palestinian love-poetry, see the Introduction. If this usage occurs here, the stich represents the closing response of the beloved, urging her lover to take his full measure of joy.

Introductory Note — 5:2 to 6:3

On the structure of this long and elaborate song, see the Introduction and Introductory Comment. Scholars who separate the song into three units, the dream-song (5:2–8), the *waṣf* (5:9–16), and the dialogue (6:1–3) (so Jastrow), or into two (5:2–7 and 5:8 to 6:3) (so Hal.), overlook the exquisite articulation of the three sections and deprive the song of much of its power. Actually, 5:8, addressed to "the daughters of Jerusalem," leads directly to their question in 5:9 and this in turn prepares for the maiden's response embodied in the *waṣf* in 5:1 ff. 6:1 then offers the natural reaction of "the daughters of Jerusalem" to the description of the lover's charms, and 6:2 her announcement that her lover has already found his way to her (so also Budde, Bettan).

The elaborateness of the contents is matched by the variety of meter. Efforts by scholars to force the entire poem into the Procrustean bed of the 3:2 *kinah* rhythm are untenable. That long poems in particular will have various meters was always clear from Biblical poetry and has been demonstrated anew by the Ugaritic epics. In our song, the *kinah* rhythm predominates, particularly in the *waṣf*, but is not the only meter employed. Its basic characteristic is that a long stich is succeeded by a shorter. Hence it may take the form of 3:2 (the most common) or a variation (3:2:2 or 4:3, or 3:3 ‖ 2:2). On the metric principles involved, see the paper cited in note 43 above.

The meter of the song is as follows:

5:2 — 4:3 ‖ 3:2 ‖ 3:3
5:3 — 4 ‖ 4 (or 2:2 ‖ 2:2)
5:4 — 4:3

5:5 — 4:3 ‖ 3:3

5.6 — 3:3 ‖ 3 ‖ 3:3 (The central stich, because of emotional impact, is an anacrusis, outside the meter.)

5:7 — 2:2:2 ‖ 3:3 (The close of the first section. Hence a longer closing distich. Accordingly, stich c, which consists of two long words, שֹׁמְרֵי הַחֹמוֹת, receives three beats.)

5:8 — 2:2 ‖ 2:2:2

5:9 — 3:2 ‖ 3:2 (The beginning of the waṣf.)

5:10 — 3:2 (To emphasize the description of the lover, the opening line has no parallel stich, adding to its force.)

5:11 — 3:2:2

5:12 — 2:2 ‖ 2:2

5:13 — 3:3 ‖ 3:3 (Stich b, מגדלות מרקחים, and stich c, שפתותיו שושנים, each receives three beats, because of the length of the words and the exigencies of the meter.)

5:14 — 3:2 ‖ 3:2

5:15 — 3:3 ‖ 2:2

5:16 — 2:2 ‖ 2:2:2

6:1 — 3:2 ‖ 3:2

6:2 — 3:3 ‖ 2:2 (Stich b, לערוגת הבשם, probably receives three beats because of its length; otherwise, the meter is 3:2 ‖ 3:2.)

6:3 — 2:2:2

5:2. The call is hardly that of a husband, estranged from his wife (against Bettan), but rather that of a lover seeking admission to his sweetheart's home.

5:4. מִן הַחֹור is extremely difficult. It is rendered by some "through the door," but the context (besides the preposition מִן) implies his withdrawal, not his opening the door. There is no need to read שָׁלַף (against Ehr., Jast.). "The hole" has been explained as a "lock" (Haupt), "window" (Siegfried), "peering-hole" (Budde), or as an obscene term for the vagina (Wittekindt, Hal.). The last view makes nonsense of the preceding verses, which are a call by the lover to be admitted to the house. The context requires an opening for the hand, not a window or peering-hole. It probably refers to an aperture through which the door can be opened from the outside. When the lover hears her negative reply, he takes it at face-value, instead of as coquetry. He therefore withdraws his hand, just as he was getting ready to let himself in. On the bowels as the seat of strong emotions in Biblical psychology, cf. Isa. 16:11; Jer. 31:19.

5:5. The myrrh dripping from her hands is taken by some to refer to the perfume which her lover had left on the door-handle (Jast., Hal.). It is better to think of her as having anointed herself with perfume before retiring, because she had expected her lover, the by-play in v. 3 being simply a flirtation (so also Ehr.). עָבַר, "dropping, dripping."

5:6. חָמַק, a pluperfect, "had gone"; cf. Jer. 31:21. נַפְשִׁי יָצְאָה בְדַבְּרוֹ is transposed by Hal. after 5a because the lover is obviously not speaking here. The correct sense of this clause, which is crucial for the understanding of the entire song, was proposed by Ehr.: "My soul passed out with longing for his speaking," or (revocalizing בִדְבָרוֹ) "for his word," i. e., "I longed to hear his voice." On the Beth = "for the sake of," cf. Exod. 10:12, נְטֵה יָדְךָ בְּאֶרֶץ, and the common *Beth pretii*. Tur-Sinai's suggestion בְדָבְרוֹ, "I went out to his pasturage" (cf. Isa. 5:17; Micah 2:12), is not only prosaic, but is ruled out by the pervasive city-background of the poem.

5:7. The city-watchmen, seeing her wandering about at night and hearing her call for her lover, mistake her for a harlot, and beat her. The cape was the outer garment, mentioned last in the "Catalogue of Finery" in Isaiah (3:23), where it may have had a more specific meaning. Jast. deletes השמרים to get a 3:2 rhythm. Besides being metrically unnecessary (see the Introductory Note), this procedure creates an unclear sense, since we would have no subject for the verbs.

5:8. מַה, literally, "what," rhetorically used, is equivalent to "that" (Ehr., Jast.).

5:10. צַח, used of shining heat (Isa. 18:4), of a milk-white complexion (Lam. 4:7), or of pure speech (Isa. 32:4), means "pure white, fair." דָּגוּל, from Akkadian *dagâlu*, "see, look upon," whence דֶּגֶל, "a flag, something visible." דָּגוּל means "outstanding, distinguished." On כַּנִּדְגָּלוֹת (6:4, 10), which is to be taken similarly, see the Commentary *ad loc.*

5:11. כֶּתֶם פָּז, rendered "fine gold," actually consists of two synonyms used for greater effect; cf. the heaping up of epithets in 4:9–10; 5:2. The change to כֶּתֶר, "crown," is attractive, but not necessary. קְוֻצּוֹתָיו, "locks." תַּלְתַּלִּים, "curled, heaped up," from תַּל, "heap." The Akkadian *taltallu* means "palm branches," a comparison to be found also in Arabic love-poetry: the hair is here conceived of as dark and wavy (Jast.).

5:12. The verse compares the dark pupil within the white iris to doves bathing in milk or perched at a clear brook. The rendering "fitly set" for יֹשְׁבוֹת עַל־מִלֵּאת (JPS) is inept. What is required is a noun denoting a pool or watering-place (so Ehr., Jast., Hal.). Tur-Sinai aptly cites Midrash Gen. Rab., section 95 (ms. Theodor), אזל למליחה, "he went to the pool where the maidens draw up the water."

5:13. מִגְדְּלוֹת מֶרְקָחִים, "towers of spices, banks of spices" (Ibn Ezra, JPS). It should be revocalized as מְגַדְּלוֹת, "raising, exuding perfumes" (so LXX, V, Tar., and most moderns), as is clear from the parallelism נֹטְפוֹת. כָּעֲרוּגַת should, accordingly, be revocalized as a plural, כַּעֲרוּגוֹת (so some Mss.), so as to supply the proper subject for the participle. Cf. 6:2 for the plural.

5:14. גָּלִיל, "rod, column." תַּרְשִׁישׁ has been identified with topaz, beryl (JPS), and rubies (Jast.). מֵעָיו, literally "reins," here represents the "skin" (Ibn Ezra, Hal.), or "the belly" (JPS). It probably refers to the entire central portion of the body. עֶשֶׁת (Akkadian išitu, "column"); cf. Ezek. 27:19. סַפִּירִים is not our sapphire, but lapis lazuli or azure, ultramarine blue in color.

6:2. It is not necessary to emend לְגַנּוֹ to לְגַנִּי or to change בַּגַּנִּים to בַּגַּנִּים (BH, Hal.).

6:4. The efforts made to identify תִּרְצָה with a famous beauty, now unknown (cf. Num. 27:1, where it occurs as a feminine proper name), and then to find another feminine name in כִּירוּשָׁלַ͏ִם, such as יְרוּשָׁא (cf. II Kings 15:33), cannot be pronounced successful. The reference is to the ancient city of Tirzah captured by Joshua (Josh. 12:24), which served as the capital of the Northern Kingdom (I Kings 14:17; 16:8, 9, 15) until it was replaced by Omri (887–876 B. C. E.) with Samaria (II Kings 16:24). While it is mentioned (II Kings 15:14) as late as the reign of Menahem, the son of Gadi (745–736 B. C. E.), its juxtaposition with Jerusalem in our song suggests that it was still the capital. Hence this lyric emanates from the half-century between Jeroboam I (933 B. C. E.) and the reign of Omri. Curiously, both the LXX and Rashi render it "a beautiful structure."

אֲיֻמָּה כַּנִּדְגָּלוֹת is a famous crux. The traditional rendering, "terrible as an army with banners" (Ibn Ezra), is hardly satisfactory. Hence it is deleted as an erroneous insertion from 6:10 (BH, Hal.). On the mythological interpretation given the phrase, when emended, in 6:10, see the Commentary there. On that view the phrase must be deleted here. Several alternatives may be suggested. The phrase may possibly be regarded as an error for אֲיֻמָּה בְּמִגְדָּלוֹת, "awe-inspiring with its towers," and it would be a description of Jerusalem. (See the Introduction on this stylistic trait of describing the simile.) This would, however, necessitate deleting the phrase in 6:10. We prefer to interpret כַּנִּדְגָּלוֹת from the Akkadian *dagâlu*, "look upon"; cf. דְּגַל, דָּגוּל, "seen, distinguished" (5:10). The MT may then be rendered: "(She is) awe-inspiring like these cynosures, great sights," literally, "things looked upon." The reference is to the cities of Tirzah and Jerusalem, just mentioned, hence the feminine plural. Thus no change in the text is required, and the same meaning is appropriate also in 6:10. The demonstrative nuance "these" inheres in the definite article, as in הַיּוֹם, "this day," כָּעֵת, "at this time," etc. Jastrow's insertion of 6:10 before 6:4, like the removal of v. 5a after v. 10 (*BH*, Hal.), is uncalled for.

6:5. הִרְהִיבֻנִי, "have frightened me" (Arabic *rahiba*, "be frightened"; Syrian *r'heb*, "tremble"). The same root seems to have, elsewhere in Hebrew, the connotation of "pride, arrogance" (Ps. 138:3; *Rahab*, the primordial beast in Isa. 30:7; 51:9). This may be an example of *'addād*, "words of like and opposite meaning." On this common phenomenon in Semitic languages, cf. Th. Noeldeke, *Beiträge zur semitischen Sprachwissenschaft* (Strassburg, 1904); Gordis, "Words of Contrasted Meaning," in *JQR*, vol. 27, 1936, pp. 33–58. For an effort to explain its origin, see *idem*, "Some Effects of Primitive Thought on Language," in *AJSL*, vol. 55, 1938, pp. 270–84. There is no need to emend to הִלְהִיבֻנִי (Ehr.), "they have enflamed me." On 6:5–7, see the Commentary on 4:1–3.

6:6. The LXX adds the first two stichs of 4:3 here, another instance of "leveling" the text.

6:8. שִׁשִּׁים הֵמָּה. The pronoun emphasizes the general statement, "There are sixty queens." הֵמָּה has been emended to לִשְׁלֹמֹה (Budde, Hal.). But since the emphasis is on the contrast between Solomon and the speaker, the word-order we should have expected is שִׁשִּׁים לִשְׁלֹמֹה מְלָכוֹת (cf. 8:11) or לִשְׁלֹמֹה שִׁשִּׁים מְלָכוֹת, not שִׁשִּׁים לִשְׁלֹמֹה מְלָכוֹת. "Twenty" is a basic number in our passage, like the English "score," so that 60 and 80, which are three and four score, respectively, represent the "ascending numeration," common in Biblical and Semitic poetry for designating a large and indefinite quantity; cf. Amos 1:3, 6, 9, 11, 13; Prov. 30:15, 18, 21, 24, 29; Job 5:19. It is therefore impossible to delete "eighty concubines" (against Jast.).

6:9. בָּרָה, not "pure" or "lustrous," but "chosen," from בור, a Mediae Vav root for the more common geminate ברר, "choose, select"; on the former, cf. Eccl. 3:18; 9:1; on the latter, see the common Mishnaic ברר. There is no need, accordingly, to invent a word בָּדָה (against *BH*). The beloved is so outstanding that her mother prefers her to all her other children, so that she is, so to speak, "one" to her mother.

6:10. אֲיֻמָּה כַּנִּדְגָּלוֹת is deleted by *BH* as an insertion from 6:4. Here again the traditional interpretation, "striking awe as a bannered host" (Jast.), is irrelevant. Dalman has suggested reading אֲיֻמָּה כַּנֵּרְגַל, "awe-inspiring like Nergal, the red star of Mars." The phrase would then be parallel with the other comparisons of the beloved to the dawn, the moon, and the sun. Even if we accept this attractive suggestion, as does Hal., it would be no evidence for the cultic use of the Song, but simply a mythological reference like those to be found in Isaiah, Psalms and Job. Several considerations, however, militate against this view: 1) It is not appropriate to 6:4, where the phrase must accordingly be deleted. 2) Not only does it require several changes in the text, but it creates a *hapax legomenon* in Hebrew. 3) While comparing one's beloved to the dawn, the sun, and the moon is understandable, to speak of her as the red star of Mars is rather strange. We accordingly prefer to interpret the phrase here exactly as in 6:4, with no change in the MT: "awe-inspiring like these great sights," literally, "these things looked upon," a participle passive of the Niphal of דגל, "gaze upon." The reference here is to the heavenly bodies mentioned before (לבנה, חמה), hence the feminine plural. See also the Commentary on 6:4.

6:11. בְּאִבֵּי הַנָּחַל, "the fresh shoots of the valley"; cf. Job 8:12.

6:12. This verse is completely incomprehensible as it stands, and as it is usually rendered, e. g. in JPS: "Before I was aware, my soul set me upon the chariots of my princely people." The LXX, V, and 20 Hebrew mss. read עַמִּינָדָב, which Budde interprets as the name of the lover or the groom. Jastrow solves the problem by regarding the verse as containing three distinct glosses, while Haupt sees in לֹא יָדַעְתִּי נַפְשִׁי the confession of a reader, "I don't understand it." But if these words are deleted as the sentiment of a reader, there is nothing left not to understand! Among the emendations proposed have been: 1) שַׂמְתַּנִי מַרְכְּבוֹת עַמִּינָדָב, "You have placed me in the chariots of Ammina-dab." 2) Graetz, followed by Hal., reads שַׂמְתַּנִי מֹרֶךְ בַּת עַמִּי נָדִיב, "You have made me fearful (literally, you have set me in fear), O nobleman's daughter." 3) Tur-Sinai brilliantly proposes to emend the phrase (and link the last three words to the next verse) to read: שָׁם תְּנִי מֹרֵךְ ‖ בַּת עַמִּי נָדִיב שׁוּבִי ‖ שׁוּבִי הַשּׁוּלַמִּית. However, attaching the two verses disrupts the rhythm of 7:1, which is normal, and is not really required. With the revocalization of our verse, as proposed by Tur-Sinai, as a basis, the passage is to be rendered: "I am beside myself with joy, for there (i. e. in the garden, v. 11) thou wilt give me thy myrrh (cf. 7:13), O nobleman's daughter." The idiom לֹא יָדַעְתִּי נַפְשִׁי apparently means "lose one's balance, normal composure," whether through great joy, as here, or through sorrow, as in Job 9:21 (Prov. 19:2 is unclear). On the reference to the beloved as "daughter of a noble kinsman" (בת עמי נדיב), or, more briefly (7:2), as "nobleman's daughter" (בת נדיב), cf. "The Dance of the Bride," in G. Dalman, *Palestinischer Diwan* (Leipzig, 1901, p. 256): "The daughter of the noble dances with two candles. Rise up, mount to the palace. By the light of thy father, precious." (Translated by Helen B. Jastrow) Arabs refer to a girl as *bint el akbar*, "Nobleman's daughter."

7:1. שׁוּבִי, either "turn" or "halt" (Ehr.). There is no need to emend to סבּי (against *BH*). מַה־תֶּחֱזוּ — "What will you see?" — is probably her modest reply, "What is there to see in me?", to which the company responds. In that event, כִּמְחֹלַת הַמַּחֲנָיִם would be their answer: "Indeed, the double — or counter dance." On the asseverative Kaph, see the Commentary on 1:7 and the references there. It is therefore unnecessary to emend the phrase to בִּמְחֹלַת הַמַּחֲנָיִם, "in the dance of two companies." It may be a reference to the sword-dance still practised by Arab brides on their wedding day. To incorporate a "military" reference in the "sword-dance," Jast. and Hal. read הַמַּחֲנִים, "camps," but this is unnecessary. הַשּׁוּלַמִּית is not a reference to the goddess Ištar (Wittekindt), nor need it be taken as the feminine of שְׁלֹמֹה, hence "Solomon's woman" (Rowley, *AJSL*, 1939, pp. 15 f.), or as the goddess Salmeiat or Shulmanitu, a Canaanite goddess of war (cf. Gaster, *loc. cit.*). Aside from the intrinsic improbability of these suggestions, the definite article indicates that the word must be a gentilic or geographical substantive; the traditional interpretation is incomparably the best: "the girl of Shulem or Shunem" (cf. Josh. 19:18; I Kings 1:3).

7:2. The spectators describe the girl, who is either naked or clothed in diaphanous veils, so that her entire person can be seen. The attention of the company is first directed to the lightning rapidity of her dancing feet and then upwards. Haupt, who inverts the order of the verses, accordingly misses the point. Ibn Ezra struggles to explain away the details of the frank description, while Kuhn interprets it as a dream. On בַּתִּ־נָדִיב, see the Commentary on 6:12. חַמּוּקֵי, "roundings, turns"; cf. Jer. 31:21; Song 5:6 for the root. חֲלָאִים, "links in a chain"; cf. Hos. 2:15; Prov. 25:12.

7:3. שָׁרְרֵךְ, "navel." אַגַּן הַסַּהַר, "bowl in the shape of a half-moon." אַל־יֶחְסַר הַמָּזֶג continues the figure of the wine goblet, "in which the mixture is not missing." See the Introduction for this stylistic usage. It is not a reference to the sperm (against Hal.).

7:5. כְּמִגְדַּל הַשֵּׁן, "like an ivory tower," because of the whiteness of the neck. Some read הַבָּשָׁן, to parallel the other geographical names in the verse, of which Heshbon is also in Transjordan. מִגְדַּל הַלְּבָנוֹן, "the tower of Lebanon," may not refer to a tower on the mountain or facing it, but to the Lebanon peak itself (Haupt, Jast.). On the standard of beauty implied, see the Introduction. צוֹפֶה, "facing toward"; cf. נִשְׁקָפָה, Num. 21:20.

7:6. כַּרְמֶל, properly "the purple land," becomes a proper noun, "the Carmel mountain"; cf. the Commentary on שָׁרוֹן (2:1). Here it is used as a common noun, like כַּרְמִיל, "crimson" (cf. II Chron. 2:6, 13; 3:14). דַּלַּת רֹאשֵׁךְ, "hair of thy head," is not compared to אַרְגָּמָן in color, but in its shining quality. Jast. points out that also in Greek love-poetry, "purple" is used to denote the rich dark color of thick hair. רְהָטִים is interpreted *ad hoc* as meaning "tresses." Its use in Ex. 2:16 as "troughs" is obviously inappropriate here, nor does Song 1:17 help us here. The root is apparently רהט (Aramaic "run"), and implies the flowing character of the long hair. Cf. 4:1; 6:5 for the figure. מֶלֶךְ = "the bridegroom"; evidence that this song describes a wedding dance.

7:7. אַהֲבָה, "love," may be a metonomy for "loved one," and there is no need to emend to אֲהוּבָה (Dal., Hal.). It is, however, best taken as an apostrophe to the love-experience itself (so Jast.). The verse elicits this enthusiastic comment from Ibn Ezra: אין בעולם תענוג לנפש ולא דבר יפה ונעים כמו החשק, "In all the world there is no such delight for the spirit and nothing as fair and pleasant as love."

7:9. סַנְסִנָּיו, "branches," from the Akkadian *sinsinnu*, "the top-most branches of the palm." A variant, with Lamed instead of Nun, occurs in Jer. 6:9, סַלְסִלּוֹת.

7:10. A very difficult verse. Stich a is obviously addressed to the beloved (וְחִכֵּךְ), while stich b would seem to be addressed by the maiden to the lover (לְדוֹדִי). The usual rendering "smoothly," for לְמֵישָׁרִים, is both unjustified and inept. For the difficult last stich LXX reads: ἱκανούμενος χείλεσί μου καὶ ὀδοῦσιν, "sufficient for my lips and teeth," which represents רַב בִּשְׂפָתַי וְשִׁנָּי (on the Greek-Hebrew equiv-alence, cf. the LXX on Num. 16:7). This probably is an erroneous rendering of a Hebrew text דּוֹבֵב שְׂפָתַי וְשִׁנָּי, a reading preferred by some commentators. Thus Hal. reads: כְּלֵיחַ שָׁרוֹן דּוֹבֵב שְׂפָתַי וְשִׁנָּי, "Like the juice of Sharon, flowing over my lips and teeth." Tur-Sinai cites the Akkadian love-charm, *ana shudbubi*, "to make the lover speak, i. e., think, of his beloved," and interprets דּוֹבֵב as a euphemism for sexual activity. The Hebrew text itself, however, needs no change. On the use of מֵישָׁרִים, in connection with wine and on its connotation of "strength, vigor," see the Commentary on 1:4. Stichs b and c, which follow the words כיין הטוב, are to be taken as descriptive of the power of wine to stimulate the strength of lovers' desire. If לְדוֹדִי

is recognized as an apocopated plural for לְדוֹדִים, "for lovers" (cf., for example, Isa. 5:1, שִׁירַת דּוֹדִי, for שִׁירַת דּוֹדִים, "a love song"; Cant. 8:2, עֲסִיס רִמֹּנִי, "juice of pomegranates"; Ps. 144:2, הָרֹדֵד עַמִּי תַחְתָּי), there is no abrupt shift of speakers and the entire verse is spoken by the lover. The verse is to be rendered: "Thy palate is like good wine, giving vigor to lovers, stirring the lips of the sleepers (with desire)." לדודים in the plural is parallel to ישנים.

Another possibility may also be suggested. The word לְמֵישָׁרִים, "for strength," may be a toast used in drinking wine, both in our passage and in Prov. 23:31, like the modern Hebrew *Leḥayyīm*, "for life," Swedish *skoal*, English "to your health," etc. Such a toast, we believe, is to be found in the Biblical יְחִי לְבַבְכֶם לָעַד, "May your hearts be alive forever" (Ps. 22:27), and דֹּרְשֵׁי אֱלֹהִים וִיחִי לְבַבְכֶם (Ps. 69:33), "Those who seek God *say*, 'May your hearts be alive!'" Our passage would then be rendered: "Thy palate is like good wine, going down for lovers with the toast 'for strength.'" The first interpretation suggested is preferable.

7:11. A reminiscence of Gen. 3:16, but radically different in spirit. There Eve is punished by being made subservient to her husband: "To thy husband will be thy desire, but he will rule over thee"; here, virtually the same words are used to express the joyous desire of the lovers for each other. On the similar use of classical Biblical texts for new ideas and attitudes in Ecclesiastes, cf. *KMW*, pp. 43 ff.

7:12. בַּכְּפָרִים, either "among the henna flowers" (Ewald, Jast., Ehr.), or "among the villages." There is no need to emend to בִּגְפָנִים (Jast.).

7:14. הַדּוּדָאִים, "mandrakes," are not only highly fragrant, but were regarded as aphrodisiacs (cf. Gen. 30:14), hence their name, derived from *dōḏ*, "lover." For דּוֹדִי, "O my beloved," it seems better to revocalize דֻּוְדִי, "My love, which I have saved for thee," taking up the theme from the end of v. 13. Verse 14a, b, c thus constitutes a parenthesis.

8:1. כְּאָח, not "like my brother," for that would not meet her problem, which is her desire to kiss her lover unashamedly in public. Nor need the Kaph be deleted (against Hal.). The Kaph is asseverative: "indeed my brother — my very brother." On this usage, cf. the Commentary on 1:7 and the references there. גַּם is adversative, "yet"; cf. Ps. 129:2, גַּם לֹא־יָכְלוּ לִי.

8:2. אֶל־בֵּית אִמִּי תְּלַמְּדֵנִי is difficult. The verb has been rendered: "that thou mightest instruct me" (JPS), but this is irrelevant here. Linking it with אַשְׁקְךָ, "she (i. e. my mother) would teach me how to make you drink," creates a harsh construction, and the meaning is dubious. The MT is explained most simply, but not quite satisfactorily, as: "to the house of my mother, who taught me." The LXX and P disregard the verb entirely and render: "to the room of her who bore me," following 3:4 (so also Dal., Hal.). It is possible that תְּלַמְּדֵנִי came into our text from a scribe, who misinterpreted וְאֶל חֶדֶר הוֹרָתִי, as in 3:4, from הוֹרָה, "teach," the Hiphil of ירה, rather than from הָרָה, "conceive," and then incorporated his erroneous synonym into the text.

Pomegranate-wine is made in lands as far apart as Persia and Mexico. רִמֹּנִי is an apocopated plural for רִמֹּנִים, which is actually the reading of some mss. and the rendering of the Targum. Cf. the Commentary on 7:10.

8:3–4. Cf. the Commentary on 2:6 f. and 3:5 and the Introductory Comment on Song XI for the interpretation of these verses and for their appropriateness here.

8:5. מִתְרַפֶּקֶת, "leaning" (JPS), "clinging" (Ibn Ezra, who cites the Arabic). חִבְּלָה, not "was in travail" (JPS), but, better, "gave birth to thee"; cf. Ps. 7:15 for the verb חָבַל and Job 39:3 for the noun חֶבֶל, "offspring." Dal. and Hal. change all the suffixes in the verse to the feminine, so as to make the entire verse an address to the beloved. While this may well be justified, it is a hazardous procedure, in view of the fragmentary and unclear nature of the passage as a whole. As it stands, it is a duet. See the Introductory Comment and the Translation.

8:6. Seals were worn on the hand (cf. Gen. 41:42; Jer. 22:24) or on a chain around the neck (Prov. 3:3; Gen. 38:18); cf. Herodotus' description of the Babylonians (I, 196). Thus they would be easily accessible, when needed for signatures on documents. In this spirit, the Torah enjoins that God's words be written "upon thy hand and between thine eyes" (Deut. 6:8), and the phylacteries worn in Jewish worship as the fulfillment of the Biblical injunction thus constitute a commentary in action on the mutual love-relationship of God and Israel. Changing the second כַּחוֹתָם to כַּצָּמִיד weakens the power of the passage (against Hal.). Nor need רִשְׁפֵּי אֵשׁ be emended to רִשְׁפֵּי אֵל (Hal.). קִנְאָה, not "jealousy," but "zeal, hence, passion," described as unyielding, never being satisfied, and hence showing no pity, like Sheol (cf. Prov. 30:15; Hab. 2:5). On שַׁלְהֶבֶתְיָה, "flame of God," as a Hebraic mode of expressing the superlative, see the Introduction and note 90, and see Gen. 10:9; Jer. 2:31; Ps. 80:11; Ps. 118:5.

8:7. The rhythm of this verse is difficult (Hal., Tur-Sinai), but it is not on that account to be regarded as prose. A verse which in isolation might well be taken for prose is to be scanned as verse if it occurs in a poetic unit. Cf., for example, Ps. 2:6, 7, the metric character of which emerges only when read in conjunction with vv. 6 and 8:

וַאֲנִי נָסַכְתִּי מַלְכִּי ‖ עַל־צִיּוֹן הַר־קָדְשִׁי

אֲסַפְּרָה אֶל חֹק ‖ ה' אָמַר אֵלַי,

בְּנִי אַתָּה ‖ אֲנִי הַיּוֹם יְלִדְתִּיךָ

Our verse may perhaps be scanned as follows:

מַיִם רַבִּים לֹא יוּכְלוּ ‖ לְכַבּוֹת אֶת־הָאַהֲבָה ‖ וּנְהָרוֹת לֹא יִשְׁטְפוּהָ

אִם יִתֵּן אִישׁ ‖ אֶת־כָּל־הוֹן בֵּיתוֹ בָּאַהֲבָה ‖ בּוֹז יָבוּזוּ לוֹ

Because of the length of the stichs לכבות את האהבה and ונהרות לא ישטפוה and the exigencies of the meter, each receives three beats. Similarly, אם and לו receive a beat. The meter is therefore 3:3:3 ‖ 3:3:3. Cf. the Introductory Commentary on 5:2 above, and the references there on the metrical principles involved.

8:8. The use of the same first person plural, both in the question in this verse (מַה־נַּעֲשֶׂה) and in the answer in v. 9 (נִבְנֶה, נָצוּר), disproves the usual view of the passage that v. 8 is spoken by the girl's brothers and v. 9 by the suitors. Actually, the suitors are putting the question and answering it (so also Tur-Sinai). On "sister" for "beloved," cf. the Introduction and 4:9 ff. Gebhardt finds two sisters here, which might perhaps prove more satisfactory to suitors, but not to the exegesis. וְשָׁדַיִם אֵין לָהּ = "not ripe for love"; cf. Ezek. 16:7–8. שֶׁיְּדֻבַּר בָּהּ = "be spoken for in marriage"; cf. I Sam. 25:39. The suitors complain, on the basis of her coldness, that she is not yet mature and ready for love and marriage.

8:9. The formula employed by the suitors follows the structure of the Oriental magic-charms (so Tur-Sinai; see the Introduction), but is purely literary here. It bears the same relationship to the genuine magical rite that a mythological reference in the Bible or in Milton bears to pagan religion. The passage is usually taken to express a contrast between the alternatives of the chastity of the maiden ("if she be a wall") and her looseness ("but if she be a door, etc."). As Tur-Sinai demonstrates, no such contrast is intended, חוֹמָה and דֶּלֶת being parallel; cf. the Akkadian ידל, "close." (The Hebrew דֶּלֶת is the infinitive of this root; cf. לָדֶת, רֶשֶׁת, from ילד, ירשׁ, respectively.) Note the Hebrew idioms דְּלָתַיִם וּבְרִיחַ (חוֹמוֹת) חוֹמָה (Deut. 3:5; I Sam. 23:7) and דְּלָתַיִם וּבְרִיחַ (בְּרִיחִים) (Jer. 49:31; Job 38:10; II Chron. 8:5; 14:6). The parallelism of חומה and דלת in our passage is well illustrated by Ezek. 38:11: כלם ישבים באין חומה ‖ ובריח ודלתים אין להם, and is clearly exhibited in the Assyrian love-charm cited in the Introduction.

Accordingly, the board of cedar is not a punishment for unchastity. The board ($lūaḥ$), like the turret ($ṭīrāh$), is a figure drawn from military operations connected with a siege. The use of "cedar" and "silver" may hint at the gifts with which the suitors hope to overcome her resistance.

8:10. The maiden's reply. Though she be a wall against her unwelcome suitors, her breasts are כַּמִּגְדָּלוֹת, "like towers." The simile does double duty. It implies that she remains impregnable to them, while her breasts are well-developed, so that she is ready for love, but only with her lover. Her constancy brings her his favor. אָז, "therefore"; cf. Jer. 22:15. כְּמוֹצְאֵת שָׁלוֹם is very difficult. It has been rendered: 1) "as a fountain of well-being." 2) "as one that has found peace" (Ibn Ezra, JPS). 3) "as one to whom good fortune comes" (Hal.). Perhaps the best rendering is 4) "as one finding grace or favor" (so Jastrow); it would then be synonymous with מָצָא חֵן. That בְּעֵינָיו refers to the would-be assailant of her virtue (Bet.) is not likely, if only because her suitors have only the honorable intention of marriage; cf. שֶׁיְּדֻבַּר בָּהּ, v. 8, and see the Commentary *ad loc.*

8:11. Though otherwise unknown, Baal Hamon (Baal Lamon in the LXX) need not be emended to Baal Hermon (Judg. 3:3). Many actual place-names do not occur in the Bible and sometimes appear in an inscription. On the other hand, it may be an imaginary locale, created to express the meaning "master of wealth." On הָמוֹן = wealth, cf. Isa. 60:5; Ps. 37:16; Eccl. 5:9; I Chron. 29:16. A vineyard which would yield produce worth a thousand pieces of silver would have a thousand vines (cf. Isa. 7:23). In Talmudic times, a tenant-farmer tilling a field received a half, a third, or a fourth of the crops as his share (B. B. 110a; Giṭ. 74b). Here the vine-tenders, נֹטְרִים (literally, "keepers"), receive only a fifth or a sixth (200 out of 1,000 or out of 1,200) for their labor. Conditions in pre-Exilic Palestine may have differed from those in Talmudic Babylonia, or, as seems more likely, farmers tilling a field would receive a greater percentage than vintners, because the work was more difficult than the tending or guarding of a vineyard. אִישׁ יָבִיא is impersonal: "any one would give"; cf. 8:7.

8:13. In accordance with the rhythm (2:2:2) and against the accents, לְקוֹלֵךְ is to be construed as the direct object of הַשְׁמִיעִנִי. On the Lamed accusative, cf. Lev. 19:18, and see the Commentary on Song 2:15.

8:14. The verse is best taken as a quotation of what the lover wants to hear (so Ibn Ezra and Hal.). Hence it is not necessary to assume a series of disjointed fragments (against Jast.). For the symbolism, cf. 2:17.

BIBLIOGRAPHY

A. TEXTS AND VERSIONS

I. *The Hebrew Text*

S. BAER and FR. DELITZSCH, Quinque Volumina (Leipzig, 1886)

C. D. GINSBURG, Masoretic Bible (London, 1st ed., 1894; 2nd ed., 1926)

R. KITTEL, Biblia Hebraica, 4th ed. (Stuttgart, 1937), edited by A. Alt and O. Eissfeldt (Masoretic notes by P. Kahle; *Canticles* edited by F. Horst)

II. *The Septuagint*

H. B. SWETE, The Old Testament in Greek (Cambridge, 1887-94)

A. RAHLFS, Septuaginta, 2 vols. (Stuttgart, 1935)

III. *Aquila, Symmachus, Theodotion*

F. FIELD, Origenis Hexaplorum quae Supersunt (Oxford, 1875)

IV. *The Vulgate*

R. STIER and K. G. W. THEILE, Polyglotten-Bibel, 4th ed. (Bielefeld-Leipzig, 1875)

V. *The Peshitta*

Kethabe Kadishe, ed. S. LEE (London, 1823)

VI. *Targum*

Mikraoth Gedoloth, Pentateuch and Megilloth (Vilna, 1912, and often reprinted)

B. SOURCES

The Hebrew Bible

The Apocrypha and Pseudepigrapha of the Old Testament (ed. (R. H. Charles, Oxford, 1913)

The New Testament—Authorized Version

Josephus, Works (Loeb Classics)

Mekilta de Rabbi Ishmael, ed. J. Z. Lauterbach (Philadelphia, 1933)

Sifre de be Rab, ed. M. Friedmann (Vienna, 1864)
The Mishnah (ed. Vilna), frequently reprinted
Tosefta, ed. M. S. Zuckermandel, 2nd ed. (Jerusalem, 1938)
Aboth de Rabbi Nathan, ed. S. Schechter, 2nd printing (New
York, 1945)
Babylonian Talmud (Vilna, 1928), frequently reprinted
Jerusalem Talmud (Krotoshin, 1866)
Midrash Rabbot on the Torah and the Megillot (ed. Vilna, 1938),
frequently reprinted
Pesikta de Rab Kahana, ed. S. Buber, 2nd ed. (Vilna, 1925)
Midrash Tehillim, ed. S. Buber (Vilna, 1891)
Pirke de Rabbi Eliezer Hagadol (Warsaw, 1862)
Tractate Sopherim, ed. M. Higger (New York, 1937)

C. COMMENTARIES

Jonah Abulwalid Ibn Janah (d. 1040), Rashi (d. 1105),
Abraham Ibn Ezra (d. 1167), David Kimhi (d. 1235), E. W.
Hengstenberg (Berlin, 1853), F. Hitzig (Leipzig, 1855), C. D.
Ginsburg (London, 1857), G. H. A. Ewald (Göttingen, 1867),
Heinrich Graetz (Vienna, 1871), Franz Delitzsch (Leipzig,
1875; English trans., Edinburgh, 1877), C. Siegfried (Göttingen,
1898), Karl Budde (Freiburg, 1898), A. Harper (Cambridge,
1907), P. Haupt (Leipzig, 1907), V. Zapletal (Freiburg, 1907),
A. B. Ehrlich (Leipzig, 1918), M. Jastrow (Philadelphia, 1921),
R. Breuer (Frankfort, 1923), G. Kuhn (Leipzig, 1926), G.
Ricciotti (Turin, 1928), C. Gebhardt (Berlin, 1931), W. Pouget
and J. Guitton (Paris, 1934; English version, New York, 1948),
M. Haller (Tuebingen, 1940), A. Cohen (London, 1946), L.
Waterman (Ann Arbor, 1948), Israel Bettan (Cincinnati, 1950),
D. Buzy (Paris, 1950).

D. GENERAL BIBLIOGRAPHY

ALBRIGHT, W. F., From the Stone Age to Christianity (Balti-
more, 1940)
———, "Palestinian Inscriptions," in J. B. Pritchard, Ancient
Near Eastern Texts Relating to the Old Testament
(Princeton, 1950)
———, "The Biblical Period," in The Jews—Their History,

Culture and Religion, ed. Louis Finkelstein, 2 vols. (New York, 1949)

————, "The Role of the Canaanites in the History of Civilization," in Studies in the History of Culture in Honor of W. G. Leland (Menasha, Wis., 1942)

BALLA, E., Das Ich der Psalmen (Goettingen, 1913)

BARON, SALO W., A Social and Religious History of the Jews (2nd ed.), vols. 1 and 2 (New York, 1952)

BEN JEHUDAH, ELIEZER, Thesaurus Totius Hebraitatis et Veteris et Recentioris, 14 vols. (Jerusalem, 1918-)

BRIGGS, C. A., The Psalms (International Critical Commentary), 2 vols. (New York, 1906)

BROWN, F., DRIVER, S. R., and BRIGGS, C. A., A Hebrew and English Lexicon to the Old Testament (Edinburgh, 1892)

BUHL, F., Canon and Text of the Old Testament (Edinburgh, 1892)

BUTTENWIESER, MOSES, The Psalms (Chicago, 1938)

CHEYNE, T. K., The Book of Psalms (London, 1888)

COBB, W. H., A Criticism of Systems of Hebrew Meter (Oxford, 1905)

COHON, SAMUEL S., "The Name of God, a Study in Rabbinic Theology," in HUCA, vol. 23 (1950-51), Part 1

CORNILL, C. H., Einleitung in das Alte Testament, 7th ed. (Freiburg, 1913)

CRAWLEY, E., The Mystic Rose (London, 1902)

DALMAN, GUSTAF H., Palestinischer Diwan (Leipzig, 1901)

————, "The Old Hebrew Calendar Inscription from Gezer," in PEFQS (1909)

DESNOYERS, L., Histoire du peuple hébreu des juges à la captivité, 3 vols. (Paris, 1922-30)

DIRINGER, D., Le iscrizioni anticho-ebraiche Palestinesi (Florence, 1934)

DORNSEIFF, F., "Aegyptische Liebeslieder, Hohes Lied, Sappho, Theokrit," in ZDMG, 1936

DRIVER, S. R., Introduction to the Literature of the Old Testament (12th ed., New York, 1906)

EBELING, E., "Aus den Keilschrifttexten," in MDOG, vol. 58 (1917)

————, "Liebeszauber im alten Orient," in MAOG, vol. 1 (1925)

————, "Aus dem Tagewerk eines assyrischen Zauberpriesters," in *MAOG,* vol. 5 (1931)

EHRLICH, A. B., Kommentar zu Psalmen (Berlin, 1905)

EISSFELDT, O., Einleitung in das Alte Testament (Tuebingen, 1934)

ENZYKLOPEDIA MIQRAIT, vol. 1, ed. by E. L. Sukenik and M. D. Cassuto (Jerusalem, 1950)

ERBT, W., Der Sternhimmel im Alten Testament (Leipzig, 1912)

ERMAN, A., The Literature of the Ancient Egyptians, trans. A. M. Blackman (New York, 1927)

FÉVRIER, J. G., "Remarques sur le Calendrier de Gezer," in *Semitica,* vol. 1 (1948)

FINKELSTEIN, L. (ed.), The Jews — Their History, Culture and Religion, 2 vols. (New York, 1949)

FRAZER, J. G., The Golden Bough (New York, 1928)

GALLING, K., Biblisches Reallexikon (Tuebingen, 1937)

GASTER, THEODORE H., "The Song of Songs," in *Commentary,* vol. 13 (April, 1952)

GESENIUS, W., and KAUTZSCH, E., Hebräische Grammatik (25th ed.) (Leipzig, 1889)

GOLDBERG, B. Z., The Sacred Fire (New York, 1930)

GOLDMAN, SOLOMON, The Book of Human Destiny (New York, 1948)

GORDIS, ROBERT, "Studies in Hebrew Roots of Contrasted Meanings," in *JQR,* vol. 27 (1936)

————, The Biblical Text in the Making (Philadelphia, 1937)

————, "Some Effects of Primitive Thought on Language," in *AJSL,* vol. 55 (1938)

————, "The Asseverative Kaph in Hebrew and Ugaritic," in *JAOS,* vol. 63 (1943)

————, "Studies in the Relationship of Biblical and Rabbinic Hebrew," in Louis Ginzberg Jubilee Volumes (New York, 1943)

————, "Al Mibneh Hashirah Haivrit Haqedumah," in *Sefer Hashanah Lihude Amerikah* 5705 (New York, 1944)

————, "A Wedding Song For Solomon," in *JBL,* vol. 63 (1944)

————, "The Bible as a Cultural Monument," in The Jews— Their History, Culture and Religion, ed. Louis Finkelstein, 2 vols. (New York, 1949)

————, "Quotations As a Literary Usage in Biblical, Rabbinic and Oriental Literature," in *HUCA,* vol. 22 (1949)

———, Koheleth—The Man and His World (New York, 1951)

———, (ed.), Max Leopold Margolis—Scholar and Teacher (Philadelphia, 1952)

GORDON, C. H., "Phoenician Inscriptions from Karatepe," in *JQR*, vol. 38 (1948)

———, "Azitawadd's Phoenician Inscription," in *JNES*, vol. 8 (1949)

GRAHAM, W. C., and MAY H. G., Culture and Conscience (Chicago, 1936)

GRANQUIST, H. N., Marriage Conditions in a Palestinian Village (Helsingfors, 1931-35)

HEMPEL, J., Die althebraeische Literatur und ihr hellenistisch-juedisches Nachleben (Wildpark-Potsdam, 1930)

HOELSCHER, G., Geschichte der israelitischen und juedischen Religion (Giessen, 1922)

HORNELL, J., "Naval Activity in the Days of Solomon and Rameses III," in *Antiquity*, vol. 21 (1947)

HUMBERT, P., Le problème du livre de Nahoum," in *RHPR*, vol. 12 (1932)

———, "Essai d'analyse de Nahoum 1:2-2:3," in *ZATW*, vol. 3 (1926)

JACOB, G., Das Hohe Lied auf Grund arabischer und anderer Parallelen neu untersucht (Berlin, 1902)

JOHNSON, BURGESS, The Lost Art of Profanity (New York,1948)

JOUON, P., Le Cantique des Cantiques (1909)

KAUTZSCH, EMIL, Die Poesie und die poetischen Bücher des Alten Testaments (Tuebingen-Leipzig, 1902)

KITTEL, R., ed., Biblia Hebraica, 4th ed. (Stuttgart, 1937)

KOEHLER, L., and BAUMGARTNER, W., Lexicon in Veteris Testamenti Libros (Leiden, 1948-)

KOEHLER, L., Theologie des Alten Testaments (Tuebingen, 1936)

KRAMER, S. N., "Sumerian Love Songs," in J. B. Pritchard, Ancient Near Eastern Texts Relating to the Old Testament (Princeton, 1950)

LESLIE, E. A., The Psalms (New York, 1949)

LIDDELL, H. G., and SCOTT, R., A Greek-English Lexicon (New York, 1883)

LIEBERMAN, S., Greek in Jewish Palestine (New York, 1942)

———, Hellenism in Jewish Palestine (New York, 1950)

Löw, I., Die Flora der Juden, 4 vols. (Vienna-Leipzig, 1924-34)

MARGOLIS, MAX L., The Hebrew Scriptures in the Making (Philadelphia, 1922)

MAY, H. G., "The Fertility Cult in Hosea," in *AJSL*, vol. 48 (1930)

MEEK, THEOPHILE J., "Canticles and the Tammuz Cult," in *AJSL*, vol. 39 (1922)

———, "Babylonian Parallels to the Song of Songs," in *JBL*, vol. 43 (1923)

———, "The Song of Songs and the Fertility Cult," in The Song of Songs—A Symposium, ed. by W. H. Schoff (Philadelphia, 1924)

MOSCATI, SABBATINO, L'epigrafia ebraica antica 1935-50 (Rome, 1951)

MOWINCKEL, S., Psalmenstudien, Nos. 1-6 (Christiania, 1921-24)

NEUSCHATZ DE JASSY, O., Le Cantique des Cantiques et le mythe d'Osiris-Hetep (1914)

NICHOLSON, R. A., Studies in Islamic Mysticism (Cambridge, 1921)

NOELDEKE, THEODOR, Beiträge zur semitischen Sprachwissenschaft (Strassburg, 1904)

———, Neue Beiträge zur semitischen Sprachwissenschaft (Strassburg, 1910)

NOTH, MARTIN, Ueberlieferungsgeschichtliche Studien (Halle, 1943)

OESTERLEY, W. O. E., and ROBINSON, T. H., History of Israel (Oxford, 1932)

OLMSTEAD, A. T., A History of Palestine and Syria to the Macedonian Conquest (New York, 1931)

PFEIFFER, R. H., Introduction to the Old Testament (New York, 1941)

POWIS-SMITH, J. M., and GOODSPEED, E. J., The Complete Bible —An American Translation (Chicago, 1943)

PRITCHARD, J. B., Ancient Near Eastern Texts Relating to the Old Testament (Princeton, 1950)

ROBERT, A., "Le genre littéraire du Cantique des Cantiques," in *Revue Biblique*, vol. 52 (1943-44)

ROWLEY, H. H., "The Interpretation of the Song of Songs," in *JThS*, vol. 38 (1937)

———, "The Song of Songs—An Examination of Recent Theory," in *JRAS* (1938)

———, "The Meaning of the Shulammite," in *AJSL,* vol. 56 (1939)

———, The Servant of the Lord and Other Essays on the Old Testament (London, 1952)

RYLE, H. E., Canon of the Old Testament (2nd ed., London, 1909) '

SALFELD, S., Das Hohelied Salomos bei den juedischen Erklärern des Mittelalters (Berlin, 1879)

SCHMIDT, N., "Is Canticles an Adonis Liturgy?", in *JAOS,* vol. 46 (1926)

SCHOFF, W. H., ed., The Song of Songs—A Symposium (Philadelphia, 1924)

SCHOTT, S., Altaegyptische Liebeslieder (Zurich, 1950)

SCHOLEM, G., Major Trends in Jewish Mysticism (New York, 1941)

SELLIN, E., Israelitische und juedische Religionsgeschichte (Leipzig, 1933)

———, Einleitung in das Alte Testament (8th ed., Heidelberg, 1950)

SPEISER, E. A., "The Contribution of M. L. Margolis to Semitic Linguistics," in Max Leopold Margolis—Scholar and Teacher, ed. by Robert Gordis (Philadelphia, 1952)

STAPLES, W. E., "The Book of Ruth," in *AJSL,* vol. 53 (1939)

STEPHAN, ST. H., Modern Palestinian Parallels to the Song of Songs (Jerusalem, 1926)

STICKEL, J. G., Das Hohelied in seiner Einheit und dramatischen Gliederung (Berlin, 1888)

TOBAC, E., Les cinq livres de Salomon (1926)

TUR-SINAI, N. H., "Shir Hashirim Asher Lishelomo," in *Halashon Vehasefer,* vol. 2 (Jerusalem, 1951)

———, "Hakethobheth Hakena 'anith Hagedolah Mi-Karatepe," in *Leshonenu,* vol. 17

VACCARI, A., I Libri Poetici della Bibbia (1925)

VON RAD, G., Das Geschichtsbild des chronistischen Werkes (Stuttgart, 1930)

VRIEZEN, TH. C., and HOSPERS, J. H., Palestine Inscriptions (Leiden, 1951)

WATERMAN, L., "The Role of Solomon in the Song of Songs," in *JBL,* vol. 56 (1936)

———, The Song of Songs Interpreted As a Dramatic Poem (Ann Arbor, 1948)

WEIR, M., A Lexicon of Accadian Prayers (London, 1934)

WETZSTEIN, J. G., "Die syrische Dreschtafel," in *Zeitschrift für Ethnologie*, vol. 5 (1873)

———, "Bemerkungen zum Hohenliede," in F. Delitzsch, Biblischer Commentar über die poetischen Bücher des Alten Testaments (Leipzig, 1875)

WITTEKINDT, W., Das Hohe-Lied und seine Beziehung zum Istarkult (Hannover, 1925)

WRIGHT, G. E., and FILSON, F. V., A Historical Atlas to the Bible (Philadelphia, 1945)

ZEITLIN, S., "An Historical Study of the Canonization of Hebrew Scriptures," in *PAAJR*, vol. 3 (1932)

INDEX OF ABBREVIATIONS

ad loc.=ad locum (to the passage)
ag.=against
AJSL=American Journal of Semitic Languages
Am.=Amos
AV=the Authorized Version (of the Old and New Testaments)

B.=the Babylonian Talmud
BASOR=Bulletins of the American Society for Oriental Research
B.C.E.=Before the Common (or Christian) Era
Bet.=Bettan
BH=R. Kittel ed., Biblia Hebraica, 4th ed.
B. S.=Ben Sira (Ecclesiasticus)

c.=circa
Cant.=Canticles (Song of Songs)
C.E.=Common (or Christian) Era
cent.=century
cf.=compare
chap.=chapter
chaps.=chapters
Comm.=The Commentary

d.=died
Dal.=Dalman
Dan.=Daniel
Del.=Delitzsch
Deut.=Deuteronomy

Ecc.=Ecclesiastes
ed.=edited, edited by, or edition
e. g.=for example
Ehr.=Ehrlich
Erub.=the tractate Erubin
Est.=Esther
Ex.=Exodus
Ezek.=Ezekiel

f., ff.=following (i.e. and the following verse [verses] or page [pages])

Gen.=Genesis

Hab.=Habakkuk
Hag.=the tractate Hagigah
Hal.=Haller
HUCA=Hebrew Union College Annual

I Chron.=I Chronicles
II Chron.=II Chronicles
1 Sam.=I Samuel
II Sam.=II Samuel
ibid.=in the same place, in the same work
ICC=the International Critical Commentary
i.e.=id est (that is)
Isa.=Isaiah

JAOS=Journal of the American Oriental Society
JBL=Journal of Biblical Literature
Jer.=Jeremiah
JNES=Journal of Near-Eastern Studies
Josh.=Joshua
JPS=The Jewish Publication Society of America Version (of the Bible)
JQR=Jewish Quarterly Review
JRAS=Journal of the Royal Asiatic Society
JThS=Journal of Theological Studies (Oxford)
Judg.=Judges

KMW=Gordis, Robert, Koheleth—The Man and His World (New York, 1951)

Lam.=Lamentations
Lev.=Leviticus
lit.=literally
LXX=the Septuagint

M.=the Mishnah
MAOG=Mittheilungen der alt-orientalischen Gesellschaft
Matt.=Matthew

107

MDMG=Mittheilungen der deutschen morgenländischen Gesellschaft
MDOG=Mittheilungen der deutschen orientalischen Gesellschaft
M. Hag.=Mishnah Hagigah
Mid.=the Midrash
ms.=manuscript
mss.=manuscripts
MT=the Masoretic text (of the Hebrew Bible)

Neh.=Nehemiah
No.=Number
Nos.=Numbers
N. T.=the New Testament
Num.=Numbers (Biblical book)

op. cit.=opere citato (in the above-cited work)
O. T.=the Old Testament

p.=page
P=the Peshitta
PAAJR=Proceedings of the American Academy for Jewish Research
PEFQS=Palestine Exploration Fund Quarterly Statement
Pes.=the tractate Pesahim
pp.=pages
Prov.=Proverbs

Ps.=Psalm

RHPR=Revue de l'Histoire et de la Philosophie des Religions
RV=the Revised Version (of the Old and New Testaments)

Sanh.=the tractate Sanhedrin
sec.=section
Shab.=the tractate Shabbath
Sym.=Symmachus

Tan.=Midrash Tanhuma
Tar.=the Targum
Tos.=the Tosefta
trans.=translated by, translation

v.=verse
V=the Vulgate
vol.=volume
vols.=volumes
vv.=verses

Wit.=Wittekindt

Yad.=the tractate Yadayim

ZATW=Zeitschrift für die alttestamentliche Wissenschaft
ZDMG=Zeitschrift der deutschen morgenländischen Gesellschaft
Zech.=Zechariah
Zeph.=Zephaniah